MY BAREFOOT DAYS

by William D. Tate

The contents of this work, including, but not limited to, the accuracy of events, people, and places depicted; opinions expressed; permission to use previously published materials included; and any advice given or actions advocated are solely the responsibility of the author, who assumes all liability for said work and indemnifies the publisher against any claims stemming from publication of the work.

All Rights Reserved
Copyright © 2023 by William D. Tate

No part of this book may be reproduced or transmitted, downloaded, distributed, reverse engineered, or stored in or introduced into any information storage and retrieval system, in any form or by any means, including photocopying and recording, whether electronic or mechanical, now known or hereinafter invented without permission in writing from the publisher.

Dorrance Publishing Co
585 Alpha Drive
Pittsburgh, PA 15238
Visit our website at *www.dorrancebookstore.com*

ISBN: 979-8-88812-113-9
eISBN: 979-8-88812-613-4

MY BAREFOOT DAYS

FOREWORD

I grew up in Grapevine, Texas, as part of a well-respected family. My paternal great-grandmother walked to Texas when she was a young mother. She was illiterate, and could not read or write, but her offspring all became very successful citizens. My maternal grandfather was Grapevine's first Night Watchman, and my father served on the school board, City Council and as mayor.

From my early developing years, as reflected in the book, I continued to grow and mature and reached high school, which became some of the best years of my life. I played wide receiver and cornerback in football and made All District Honorable Mention my senior year. I also played basketball and was the co-captain of my team and made All District that last year. I was named school favorite and received the Citizenship Award at graduation. I went to Austin College and played basketball one year but my ankles were breaking down and causing so much pain I had to give the sport up. I transferred to North Texas State University where I graduated with a BBA degree with majors in accounting and education. I worked at a public accounting firm in Dallas while I was going to law school at the University of Houston. After receiving my Doctor of Jurisprudence Degree, I went to work full time for the accounting firm and started working towards my CPA, which I never finished. After my dad died suddenly at the age of 58, I opened my law office in Grapevine where I could also help manage my parents' stores on Main Street, where I grew up. In 1969 I was appointed City Attorney by the City of Grapevine and served three years before being elected to the City Council. After my first year on the council, the mayor decided not to run again, and encouraged me to run in his place. I was only 30 years old at the time and was elected mayor by a large majority. I have been mayor of my hometown for 47 years now and am the longest serving mayor in Texas and the third longest serving mayor in the United States

Soon after I became mayor, the Dallas Ft. Worth International Airport opened taking approximately 40% of land mass off the tax rolls. Only about a third of our land was taxable because the rest was owned by tax exempt governments, schools, churches or other non-taxable entities. I had to find a way to finance and transform a small agricultural town into an international city. We developed a business plan based on sales taxes and hospitality. Today we have the second lowest tax rate in Texas of cities over 50,000 population. Our historic Main Street survived the coming of Walmart and we placed overlay ordinances on our historic residential district which also has survived the test of time. Citizens have moved here from every state in the Union and many foreign countries and they live together on wooded lots as friends and family, and most volunteer in our community making it an enjoyable place to live and work.

I have been honored in many ways. I received the Citizen of the Year Award, named to Grapevine High School Hall of Fame and Walk of Honor, received the Boy Scouts of America Silver Eagle Award, the Hospitality Industry Development Award from the Texas Travel Industry Association, Daughters of the American Revolution Community Service Award, Honorary Commissioner of Tarrant County, Who's Who in Texas, named Distinguished Southern by *Southern Living* Magazine, the Ted Willhoite Legacy Award and Texas Hotel & Motel Association Hospitality Hero Award, a Lifetime Achievement Award from the Greater Fort Worth Builders Association, Abilene Christian University Parents of the Year, voted several times the Best of the Best Local Government Official, and a major thoroughfare bears my name.

I have been married for over 53 years and have five daughters all of whom became teachers. I have fifteen living grandchildren and two more who died too soon. My family history and my own life are sure proof that by working hard and going for the gold, you can overcome your limitations and find success in life, proving once again that America is the land of opportunity.

PREFACE

In my sixtieth year, I decided that the time was ripe for me to reduce to writing a physical description of the indelible photos that I carry around in my mind, of the cherished days of my childhood, all spent in Grapevine, Texas. The community was only a village when I first arrived with a night watchman as the only city employee. I have since seen it mature into a town, then a city, then one of the brightest stars in the constellation that we now call the DFW Metroplex.

The early settlers were primarily products of the Peter's Colony who came from Missouri in 1844, followed by settlors disheartened by Civil War, who came during or after Reconstruction from Tennessee, Georgia, Alabama, Arkansas, Kentucky, Ohio, Illinois and other states, bringing with them a ragbag of hopes and their belief in God. They came in search of peace, fortune and a better life for themselves and their families. I came from the best of their breeding and am a product of the blending of their pioneer spirit, hard work, and determination.

I find their individual stories compelling and see myself as one of the grateful benefactors of their accomplishments and survival. I am saddened only by the knowledge that my childhood represents a way of life gone forever, one that will never be repeated in America.

Throughout my life I have watched the settlers continue to arrive from every state in the union and many foreign countries. We have here a diverse community, and with the arrival of just a few hundred more settlers, the gates will slam shut and our population will reach build out.

William D. Tate

    I hope that those who founded this community on the promise of good fortune, cheap land, and new beginnings, who sweated, sacrificed, and watched the pages of history turn from generation to generation, will be proud of what has been accomplished here since they left the earth. The final configuration is nearly complete, for the conversion of the Grapevine Prairie into bricks and mortar and a poverty economy replaced by a more effluent society.

    I will never forget the days of my innocence, the influence of my parents and grandparents, and the encouragement I received from my sister, who became a teacher and a historian. My family continues to grow, with a wife and five daughters, all teachers, and a gaggle of son in laws and grandkids, accomplishing one thing for sure if nothing else: In the name of the Lord, I've spread the seeds of Abraham over this rich, black soil that I've called home.

    I never dreamed that when I started that it would take me eighteen years to write the first one third of the chapters, and then while being home shuttered during the Covid-19 Pandemic, that it would only take me eighteen days to finish the book. Looking back, some might think my childhood was a social bore, as compared to the gadget generation of today. But for others who will take the time to read the book, I hope you find it interesting and worthwhile as you reflect upon the "make do with what you had" generation that has been mine.

DEDICATION

My sister was my only sibling growing up and she had a profound impact on my life. She blazed new trails for me and dragged me along the path behind her. She introduced me to things that she experienced first because she was older. She taught me how to ride a bicycle, dance, how to drive a car and what movies to go see. She taught me how to respect women and how they could contribute to our society. She was my biggest supporter and enjoyed the history of our community as much as I do. I dedicate this childhood book to my beloved sister, Sandra Kay Tate, in appreciation of her support, her impact on my life, and the memories that we generated together.

TABLE OF CONTENTS

1. My Arrival 1
2. Milk Bottles and Watermelons. 1
3. Stillborn. 3
4. When the Soldiers Came Home 4
5. The Stores. 5
6. Water Stains and New Car. 8
7. Grand Dad and Grand Ma Bennett 8
8. A Child's Prayer and Moonlit Nights 9
9. Toy Box and Rocky Horse 11
10. Ice Boxes and Homemade Ice Cream 11
11. Caster Oil and Croup. 13
12. Rub Boards and Churns. 13
13. The Cellar and Stormy Nights. 15
14. China Berries and Sling Shots 16
15. The Cat Carried It Off 18
16. Church and Sunday School. 19
17. Setting Hens and Bantams. 20
18. Bedrolls and Painted Nails 22
19. Shoe Shopping and Rude Awakenings 23
20. Domino Games and Smoke 24
21. Pecan Trees and Other Fruits. 25
22. The Garage. 27
23. The Barn. 28
24. Mud Pies and Sprinklers 30
25. Picket Fences and Trails 31
26. Gardens and Earthworms 32
27. Brooms and Belts 34

28. Stocking Shelves and Inventories. 35
29. Dollie Berry and Mr. Charlie. 36
30. Attics and Those Sorts of Things 38
31. Grass Mowing and Flowers. 39
32. Poetry and Prose 40
33. Tar Trucks and Fogging Machines. 41
34. Horse Apples and China Berries. 42
35. Doodle Bugs, Mud Pies and Old Wells. 43
36. Case Knives 43
37. Pole Vaulting and Telephone Wires 44
38. The Backyard Tree. 45
39. Barn Owls and Hackberry Trees. 46
40. Orion and the Stars 47
41. Swings and Smokestacks. 47
42. Jones Street and West End. 48
43. I Loved Flowers 50
44. Cub Scouts and Weebolos 51
45. Christmas Trees and Candy. 52
46. Santa Claus and Presents 53
47. Ice in the Water Bucket 56
48. Pathfinder and Flowersack 56
49. Bible Schools and Washtubs 57
50. BBs, Revolvers and a 4l0. 58
51. Old Dogs and Water Barrels. 59
52. Cowboys and Indians 60
53. Piano Lessons and Recital 61
54. The Crepe Myrtle Tree 62
55. Rabbits and Homemade Cages 63
56. Saturday Drawings and Coupons. 64
57. The Wizard of Oz 64
58. Porch Swings and Summer Evenings 65
59. Pottery and Birdbaths 66
60. Vitex and Badminton 67
61. Water Fans and Sheets 68
62. Bicycle Paths and Sidewalks. 69
63. The Sheds. 70
64. Mrs. Parr and ABC's. 71
65. Back to School and Wild Geese 72
66. Recess and Swings 74
67. Water Fountains and Bicycle Racks 74

68. Family Reunions 75
69. Basketball Goals 78
70. Mur's House and Baby Chicks 79
71. The Old Iron Bed 80
72. Circus Pony and Figure Eights 81
73. Pig Pens and Show Hogs 82
74. Curing Meat and Smoke Houses 83
75. Quail Dogs and Picking Peas 84
76. Crows and Crow Calls 85
77. Cardboard Boxes and Puppets 86
78. Learning to Fish 87
79. Intenerate Veterinarian 89
80. Oatmeal Boxes and Crystal Sets 90
81. Crawdads and Fishing Holes 91
82. Ducks and Such 92
83. Fireplaces and Chimney Swifts 93
84. Playmates 94
85. Golden Books and Rudolph 95
86. Firecrackers and Roman Candles 96
87. Birthday Cakes and Measle 97
88. Muffins, Hot Rolls and Cookie Jars 98
89. House Fires and Making Kites 99
90. By the Oz or by the Pound 100
9l. Exterminators and Floor Sweep 101
92. Bumble Bee and Vacations 102
93. Football games and Homecoming 103
94. First and Second Deer Hunt 104
95. The Basket Factory 105
96. The Bachelor 106
97. Peanuts and Cracker Jacks 107
98. Cheerios and Shredded Wheat 108
99. Swimming Holes 109
100. The Secret Room 110
101. Shows at Will Rogers Auditorium 11
102. Dressing up was Hard to Do 112
103. Post Office and Comic Books 112
104. Our Summer Bedroom 113
105. Chicken, Pork and a Side of Beef 115
106. Radios and Television 115
107. Floursacks and Bins 116

108. Drive-In & Submarine Races 117
109. Parades and Carnivals 118
110. Harris Hatchery & Baby Chicks. 119
111. Releasing fish & Boat Building 119
112. Candling Lighting & Mistletoe 121
113. The Big Scare. 121
114. City Services & Fire Trucks 122
115. Saturday Drawings and Coupons 123
116. Cotton Sacks & Bracero's 124
117. Banana Stalks and Cold Drinks 125
118. Mason Jars & Tin Cans. 125
119. Charge Accounts & Counter Checks 126
120. Quail Picking and Churning 127
121. Granddad Tate and Cherry Springs. 128
122. Filing Stations and Fixing Flats 129
123. Saturday Afternoon Matinee 130
124. Donkey Ball Games and Globe Trotters 130
125. Womanless Weddings and Cake Walks. 131
126. Valentine Box and Easter Egg Hunt. 132
127, The Night Fires. 133
128. Drive-In and Submarine Races. 134
129. Flashbulbs and Family Movies 135
130. Apple Crates and Orange Boxes 136
131. Magic and a Bag of Tricks. 136
132. Summer Lunch. 137
133. Cemeteries and Holiday Flowers 137
134. Minature Golf and Avocado Seed. 138
135. The Night Watchman 139
136. Civil Defense and Space 140
137. Strawberry Sodas and Comic Books 140
138. Record Players and Barn Dances 141
139. Halloween and Outhouses 142
140. Crickets and Grasshoppers 142
141. The Anvil and Molasses 143
142. Drilling of the Water Well 144
143. Little League and Ball Fields. 145
144. Model Airplanes and boomerangs 145
145. The Parakeet 146
146. The Last Days for Grand Dad 147
147. Coming of Age 148

148. Learning to Drive 149
149. Thunder and Lightning 150
150. The Wiley's. 151
151. The Plane Crash. 153
152. The First Kiss and Spinning the Bottle 153
153. The Dutchman. 155
154. The Fort Mason Hotel 156
155. Church Camp and Grapevines 157
156. Dove Hunt and Chiggers. 158
157. Snow and Ice Storms 158
158. Pencils and Paper. 159
159. Homemade Clothes and Chattering Teeth 160
160. The Gangsters 161
161. Groundbreaking and Dedication 162
162. Shaving my Dad 163
163. Cotton and the Garbage Truck 164
164. The Old Men of the Stores 165
165. Incubator and Quail. 166
166 Raising Quail 167
167. Allison's Clinic 168
168 June bugs and fireflies. 169
169. Entertained by the Prairie 170
170. Butcher Blocks and Meat Grinders. 171
171. Arrowheads and Indians. 171
172 Picture Stump 173
173. Evading Polio 173
174. Encyclopedia and Reference Books. 174
175. Don't Ever Forget Him. 175
176. Hobos and Dark Nights. 176
177. The Barrow Gang 176
178. My Own Grandpa 178
179 Junior High. 179
180. Railroad and Depot 181
181. Barefoot Days and Sandburs 182

1. MY ARRIVAL.

I was born on May 11, 1942 at Methodist Hospital in Fort Worth, Texas, the second child born to Gordon Douglas Tate and his wife Annie Louise Tate. My parents brought me home a few days later to live my life and grow up with my sister Sandra Kay Tate in the family homestead at 218 W. College, Grapevine, Texas. It was the house that my Bennett grandparents built and was where my mother grew up. It was a copy of the house of another family member who lived in San Antonio. I weighed ten pounds at birth. Like my sister when she was born, I had no hair. That would soon change. As the first months of my life passed, I began to sprout a lot of blond, curly hair that my mother adored. My childhood years and experiences represent what it was like growing up in a small farming community that had evolved out of the pages of history. Grapevine is the oldest surviving community in Tarrant County, Texas, founded in 1844, under the flag of the Republic of Texas, by a group of Scottish-Irish settlers from Missouri, who had lost everything they had in the floods of the Missouri River and walked to Texas to claim free, fertile land on the Grapevine Prairie. They defeated danger, faced and defeated disease and hardship, and were able to carve out of the wilderness a new beginning. These brave and determined men and women laid the cornerstone of our community, and gave us a name and a place to call home.

2. MILK BOTTLES AND WATERMELONS

I nursed the bottle until I was three years old. My mother was afraid it was going to give me buckteeth and she might have been right. She had taken some kind of chalk like medicine when she was pregnant to give me good teeth, and she didn't want to have a reversal of fortunes. When Mother finally hid the baby bottle in the upper kitchen cabinet, where I could not climb or reach, I gave up on milk. I never did like it much the rest of my childhood, except on cereal.

I can remember the bottle well. It was my pacifier. I remember lying in my baby bed, that was against the wall in the back bedroom, or lying on one of the big beds and taking my bottle so I would go to sleep for a nap. It got where it wouldn't work, because I didn't like to take naps and that wasn't going to change. If I had been smart enough to keep going to sleep, I could have probably held on to that bottle another couple of years.

I can remember having my diaper changed and being placed in my crib at night. I can also remember trying to learn to walk and being potty trained and how frustrating it was. My parents would bring the little potty chair into the middle bedroom and make me sit on it even though I didn't need to poop. I remember my Aunt Martha Snow coming to visit, and sitting in her lap and watching her draw ducks, fish, dogs, birds, and other animals for me on a piece of paper. That was a happy time. I remember other friends and relatives that came to visit and wanted to hold me, but I never liked to be held that much. I remember them talking about me having green eyes and how rare that was for a boy. Green eyes, they said, "were usually reserved for a red hair girl."

My grandfather Bennett had a milk route around town and delivered bottle milk before we had refrigerators. He delivered it in milk cans by horse and buggy. Mother was used to having a milk cow and so was Dad since he grew up on a farm, so we had a milk cow most of the time when I was little. But, Mother bought me pasteurized milk in the store or condensed milk; she wouldn't dare give me milk from the cow. The home milk was used for cooking and for making butter.

My dad liked watermelons. He was always bringing one home from the store, and we would eat it Sunday afternoon out in the backyard under the big hackberry tree. They would strip me down to my diaper or panties and give me a big, long slice. I would just eat and let the juice roll down my cheeks, elbows, and stomach. I would spit the seeds out, but sometimes it was just easier to eat them too. They don't make watermelons anymore like those big Black Diamonds that could grow to 100 lbs. When my sister and I were through eating watermelon, our parents would turn the water hose on us and wash us down.

One year my dad found a farmer near Paradise who had Black Diamond watermelons growing volunteer in his corn patch. You could pick them yourselves for ten cents a piece. Dad made several trips and I made a few with him. They were sixty and seventy pounders, and more than I could carry. Every once in a while, I would pick one up off the ground high enough to drop and crack it open. Dad taught me how to run my fist all the way up in the middle and pull the seedless heart out. Boy, even on a hot day the meat would be a little cool and the juice refreshing running down your chin. Dad said that was the very best way to eat watermelon.

We would load our 1949 green Chevrolet pickup up to the top of the bed and head for Grapevine. Dad would back the truck bed first in front of grocery store. We had head in parking back then. I would sell them right off of the truck on a Saturday afternoon for twenty-five cents apiece. At a quarter a piece, they wouldn't last long.

3. STILLBORN

The war with Japan was drawing to a conclusion though the atom bombs had not been dropped yet. My mother was pregnant with a third child. I had been moved out of the baby bed into the big iron bed with my dad to make room for the new baby. As time for delivery approached, my mother moved in with her sister, my Aunt Lela Mae Wiley, who lived on Honeysuckle Street in the Oakhurst District of Fort Worth, so she would be near Methodist Hospital. She went into labor on May 10, 1945, the day before my third birthday. Her doctor was her cousin, Dr. Jerrell Bennett, who had also delivered my sister and me. The doctor gave my mother some codeine, which she turned out to be allergic to. Before delivery they told my mother that there was no heartbeat and the baby was delivered "still born." It was a boy, with a lot of dark hair, and he was given the name Don Richard Tate. My Aunt Mary Ruth Tate took a few pictures of him, but my mother never looked at them. Mother never saw the baby, who is buried in Grapevine Cemetery. It was not discussed at home. I never knew that I had a brother until I read in my Bible years later. My mother had a tough time after she lost the baby and had a nervous breakdown because she thought the codeine killed the baby. I knew my mother was sick, but I didn't know why. A lady stayed in the house for a while and helped her recover. I can remember my mother crying a lot when I was growing up. She never did get over the death of her third child. Don Richard's birthday was the day before mine, and every birthday I had was a reminder to her of her loss. I guess that is why my birthday celebrations were few and far between. I often wondered what life would have been like if the baby had lived.

4. WHEN THE SOLIDERS CAME HOME

I can remember when the soldiers started coming home after WWII. Some came home by bus and some by rail. Some had to be picked up in Fort Worth. In other instances, relatives travelled to see loved ones who came back on ships on the West Coast. They didn't arrive all at the same time, but there was a big celebration with each return. My Uncle Clois Tate and Uncle Erman Tate came home at different times. Clois had been in the military police, an MP, and did not get to come home as quickly as those who had been on the front lines. Clois was unmarried and moved home with his parents. I remember his uniform and nap sack and when he was back in our lives. My Uncle Erman had been in the Navy and wore their blue and white uniforms. He was a medic and served during the war on a ship. He was married and had two children. One of my dad's cousins, Jimmy Tate, was shot down and killed in a plane when he was nineteen years old; I often saw his grave at Flower Mound when we went there to tend the graves. It was only a marker, because his body was lost at sea. Both of my uncles came home smokers. They had been given free cigarettes because they were good therapy for their nerves.

The ex-soldiers started coming into the local hardware store to sit around in the guest chairs and talks about their hopes and aspirations and also their disappointments. I sat and listened day after day and learned a lot from their wisdom. After a time, I made a commitment to myself that I would live my life in such a way that when I was forty, I could say, "I'm glad I did." That I would not have to be one of those sad souls who had to say, "I wish I had."

I learned a lot about life from these men who had suffered many hardships and had seen so much horror. They talked a little about war, how it involved them or how they were wounded and the time it took to recover. I remember hearing about the German hedge rows, and how many Americans had died in the fire fights there. I remember the news reels that showed the hedge rows around fields in France and Germany, and I could easily imagine how well the enemy could hide and surprise you from that vantage point.

I remember going to Dallas and riding the trolley to the Veterans Hospital to see the husband of my mother's cousin Charles Pangburn, who was recovering from wounds that he received just after the war ended when he was walking the beach. He stepped on some kind of explosive that detonated and injured his legs. After he arrived home, he had to spend more time in the hospital recovering.

Soon the money that had gone into the war effort was invested in new housing, and the retail market was flooded with new devices to make like more convenient like electric washing machines and dryers, televisions, electric shavers, and toasters. The construction of the Grapevine Lake was started on land which had been surveyed prior to the war, and Bellaire Addition and the Box Addition were developing and gaining momentum. Cameron Co. Lumber Yard had modern house plans, and designed and built new frame box houses with low roofs. It was a time of great growth and celebration as people enjoyed life to the fullest. B & D Mills was expanded and became the largest employer, a new high school was built, and new water well drilled at the corner of Main and Hudgins Street. Grapevine was growing everywhere you looked, and there was great anticipation of the change the lake would bring to our community.

5. THE STORES.

My father and grandfather Tate owned and operated the Tate Cash Stores. There was a grocery store and hardware store in the 400 block of Main and the furniture store was across the street next to the City Hall. It all started in 1937 when dad and my granddad left Buckner's to go into business for themselves. Granddad was a butcher for Buckner's and found out he was going to get fired and so both my dad and granddad left and went into competition with Buckner's. My granddad was a jokester and sometimes quick-witted, which might have got him in trouble. The first business started in just half a building with groceries and then spread into the entire building at 420 Main. The hardware was started later in the building to the north when it became available. It was once the Farmers State Bank.

The grocery had a storage area in back and also a balcony where merchandise and supplies were stored. There was a single restroom in the back.

There were two large back doors that opened in where merchandise was delivered. They were closed at night and secured from the inside by a two by four that slipped through metal brackets on each end. There was a large sink in the back where the market equipment was cleaned and a large hot water heater. The upstairs balcony could only be reached with a built in ladder. A platform scale in the back weighed large objects. A thin wall separated the back storage from the rest of the store. The meat market was just on the front side of this wall, and the milk case and vegetable cases were to the right of the meat. The brooms and mops were clipped on a wire hanger that hung from the ceiling. The office was located in the back corner as was a large safe. The aisles ran from the front door east and west the length of the building to the back partition. Everything always had its place, and we never changed where each product was located. There were two display windows up front where sales and merchandise was advertised. On the south wall was the cereal and Jell-O, baking powder, and artificial flavorings and spices. In the next aisle were the cold drink case, bread rack, and cookie rack. Next aisle held the cash register and checkout station that had the cash register on one end. Sacks were held in metal bins overhead and in the back was the charge account cabinet. Underneath the check-out were the sugar and snuff.

On the other side of the check-out counter were the cigarettes, candy case, and ice cream. Across the aisle were the school supplies, tissue paper, and paper towels. The next aisle had medicines and pharmaceutical products, flour, and meal. Then on the north wall were the soups, canned milk, can goods vegetables, and dog food. We had wire handle baskets that customers used to gather groceries until the rolling baskets came out. The building was heated by a large gas stove in front and a smaller one in the meat market. It was cooled by a large attic fan that set on top of the balcony and pulled air from the back door through the store. We rented the building from Huber and Ruby Lipscomb.

The hardware store was next door at 418 Main. It had three large display windows and window boxes to display merchandise. There were no awnings and the sun destroyed or at least faded any merchandise that was left in the window for very long, so it had to be constantly redone. Dust collected in the displays from the street, another reason to replace the window displays. Most people coming to the hardware parked out back and came through the back door. Entering the store, they found hoes, racks, shovels, post hole diggers, and the like around the north wall. That store also had a balcony with a stairway where we stored merchandise. In the back were the pipe fittings and plumbing products, as well as screws and bolts. The rope was underneath the electrical table where the wiring was kept, measured and sold by the foot. There was a partition that separated the front from the back of the store, just like in the grocery store. In the front we had the nails that we weighed by the pound on a scale that hung from the ceiling. On the west wall we had the tack and bridles, the stove pipe, garbage cans, buckets, wash tubs and wash pots, wood and kerosene stoves, hardware cloth, and screen wire that we measured and sold. In the corner was the seed bin where we sold seed by the pound and by the ounce. On the front along the south wall was the Fixall paint; then came the springs and hinges, the files, and etc. Beginning with the next aisle was two counters of cooking utensils and dishes, the next aisle with Dupont paint, and then the electrical counter with all of the electrical switches, plates, fuses, breakers, plug, connectors and related products. In the middle front was the cash register and checkout counter. The telephone set on a shelf. Next to the telephone was the wrapping counter. A large mahogany counter stored large seed, like English peas, corn and beans that we sold in bulk. On top were the scales and a role of brown paper that we wrapped products, next to it was the seed potatoes in season and ice chest, bailing wire, and water cans. Along the north wall towards the front were the gun cabinet, ammunition and hunting supplies, the gopher traps, oil lamps and globes, footballs, basketballs, sport shoes then in the next aisle was the fishing equipment and lures. Next to it was a counter that had gloves and hardware products. The next aisle towards the center had the hand tools and another cabinet had fishing reels, knifes, paean sheller, and etc.

The building was cooled by an evaporated cooler that was over the back door and sent air down the center aisle. We set products out on the sidewalk each morning in front of the hardware and grocery and brought them in at closing time…things like bicycles, red wagons, plows, water cans, tomato plants, pepper plants and flowers.

There was a gas stove up front with cane bottom chairs for customers to sit and visit and they were used a lot. It was a meeting ground for the men of the town. This is where I heard their dreams and disappointments and aspirations for the community.

The furniture store was not open except when we wanted to show products like linoleum rugs, joints of pipe, refrigerators, stoves, washing machines, etc. We sold a lot of twenty-foot joints of galvanized or black pipe in 1/2 inch, ¾ inch, 1 inch and 1l/2. Usually we wired the pipe underneath the customer's car or truck with bailing wire. We later split the building and leased the south side to Texas Power and Light Co.

6. NEW CAR AND WATER STAIN

When the 1948 Chevrolet sedans came out, they came in colors other than black. My dad bought a new car that was green outside with a tan interior. He was very proud of this car. One day when it was new, he was driving it to Fort Worth to serve on a federal grand jury after a big rain. When he approached the underpass at the Cotton Belt Railroad, with the driver's window open, another car passed him and sprayed water and mud inside the roof of the car. It also got my dad wet and dirty, so he had to return home and change clothes. He was just sick over the incident. After the mud dried in the car, it was brushed off, but we could always see the mark where it had been. We kept this car for about ten years. It was a constant reminder to keep the windows closed even though it did not have air conditioning.

7. GRANDDAD BENNETT

My maternal granddad, William Madison Bennett, gave me my first name as did my paternal great-grandpa Will Nowlin. He was the son of Mr. and Mrs. Henry Harrington Bennett, former resident of Tennessee, who settled near Coppell upon coming to Texas in 1866. He was converted at the age of 15 and has been a devoted Christian since that time. He married Etta Elizabeth Willingham on December 10, 1896. Mr. Bennett was a farmer who lived on a 120-acre farm in Coppell until the early 1900s when he moved to Grapevine with his wife Etta and his daughter Lela Mae Bennett. They bought a house on West College Street in Grapevine that had been built in 1888. Here his second daughter was born, Annie Louise Bennett who would become my mother. Granddad Bennett became the first night watchman of the town, being elected as City Marshall in 1907. He was also involved in the Methodist Church in town and served as its superintendent. He was religious, pious, and scriptural. He moved the house a half a block to 507 Church Street and built in its place at 218 W. College Street, a new home that was a replica of his sister's home in San Antonio, Texas. This is the home where my mother grew up, went to school, and would later live a big part of her life with my dad Gordon Tate and my sister Sandra and me.

Granddad Bennett never had time to foolishly idle away a moment. He tried to make every moment count for something and for something that was worthwhile. He mastered many things in life. He had a sense of the beautiful. We could see this by the care that he took of his homes and of the church. He always desired to make the church more attractive for others to come for spiritual food. He never departed from the high standards that were his ideals that were radiated through his daily life. He was always doing something for others and could always be depended upon.

He later became a member of the staff at the Grapevine Post Office and would go to the depot in a horse and buggy with my mother to pick up the bags of mail that were dropped by the trains that ran the Cotton Belt Line. He was well respected in the community. He kept the farm in Coppell, Texas, which he rented to a sharecropper. He also raised Persian horses. Granddad Bennett never knew my sister or me because he died at the age of 62 in 1936, after a short illness. That was the year that Texas would celebrate its Centennial. Before he died in the house at 218 W. College Street, the last thing he said when he heard the nine o'clock train was, "That is the last train headed east."

8. A CHILD'S PRAYER AND MOONLITE NIGHTS

Above the baby bed was a green cardboard that had written in gold the words of the *Child's Prayer*. It was framed and decorated with cupids and angels around the edges. When I was in my crib, I would stand and look up on the wall before I went to sleep each night and my mother read to me the words. I, of course, couldn't read but looked at the characters. I stayed in the baby bed until I was three. The new baby would displace me from my bed. When the baby was born dead, my parents took down the baby bed, and it disappeared. My dad probably sold it to someone that needed a baby bed, because I don't ever remember seeing it again.

I moved into the big iron bed that my dad slept in and my Granddad Bennett before him. It was always painted gold. It was moved around in the back bedroom from spring to winter, but after the baby bed was gone it was left in the same corner of the room. There were big windows all along the north side of the room, one on the west and two big ones on the east. From my advantage point in the bed, I could look out the window at night and see the sky the house next door, together with the picket fence that began at the corner of the house.

I could always see the stars, even though the big hackberry in the back yard had limbs that encroached over the edge of the house. Each month I watched the moon get larger and larger, and then get smaller and smaller. I am sure I asked my parents about this phenomenon. I would lie in bed, and look out the window, before I would go to sleep. I thought a lot. I watched the trees blowing in the wind, especially in the winter, and listened to the noise that their branches made while I watched the shadows that they cast. I watched the man in the moon rise right over the Lipscomb house and climb into the night sky. I remember how big and orange the harvest moon would be in the fall. I hadn't heard about the red moons or pink moons, or Comanche moons, Harvest moon, or the other names that the moon was called.

In summer we would have the windows open for ventilation. I could hear and see the June bugs and grasshoppers on the window screens yearning to get in. I would take my finger and thump them off the screen. There were so many kids in my parent's generation that died in the days of their youth, that to me prayer was an important communique with God. My father had a sister that died at three months and another one that died at six months from the milk fever. So, the thought of a child dying was always on every parent's mind. It was not too many years before I could recite the *Child's Prayer* myself which I did every night. I would stand at the head of the bed before I lay down and hold the metal post of the bed and jump up and down as I read the *Child's Prayer*. "Now I lay me down to sleep, I pray the Lord my soul to keep, and if I die before I wake, I pray the Lord my soul to take."

9. TOY BOX AND ROCKY HORSE

I slept in the back bedroom which was my father's room. My mother's room was next door so she could hear me in the night. Across the room in the northeast corner was a large red toy box. It was filled with toys, but I had to lean over and nearly fall in the box to reach the playthings. I had a teddy bear that I kept on the bed, but the box stored things like trains, a stick horse, wood blocks, puzzles, tinker toys, Lincoln logs, and my shooting game that came with black crows and a gun with a cork. The toy box had a lid that slid shut so that I could sit on top. I soon had more toys than the toy box would hold. Like the baby bed, the toy box disappeared one day. I never knew where it came from or where it went. My father was a merchant, and he would sell anything and everything, so I guess like my baby bed, my dad had a customer that wanted to buy a toy box and he sold it. This was not until I had outgrown these type of toys, moving on to more sophisticated ones like BB guns and sling shots.

My sister had a rocky horse and when she got upset, she would get on the rocky horse and ride as hard as she could. It was a good therapy for her growing up. When she out-grew the rocky horse, then I started riding it myself. It had springs on it so you could get a lot of action. Remembering how my sister had ridden it, I ended up doing the same thing, trying to ride the horse into the ground as if I was chasing an outlaw.

10. ICEBOXES AND HOMEMADE ICE CREAM

My parents had a furniture store, so when the refrigerators first arrived in our town, we got one real fast. But I remember the old icebox and the ice truck that came around every couple of days to bring a block of ice to keep the icebox cool. The iceman had a leather apron that he wore strapped on his back and carried an ice pick in a leather holster on his belt. He carried the ice with a great big pair of silver hooks that would open wide around the ice. When he pulled up on the handles, the hooks would dig into the ice. They were called thongs. It made a nice handle to carry the ice from the truck into the house to keep the ice clean and from freezing the ice man's hands. The ice man then took an ice pick and cut the ice into the size of block needed for each customer, usually 25 or 50 pounds.

I liked to follow the ice man when he came to into our neighbors houses to see how much ice they would need, so I would visit a lot when the ice man was in our neighborhood. You could buy ice on Sunday at the Grapevine Ice Plant located on Northwest Highway. It sold block ice or crushed ice for things like home made ice cream or cooling down watermelons or soft drinks. The icehouse had an employee who would go into the cold storage and get whatever amount of ice you wanted. Later there was a coin-operated vending machine where you could buy 25 pounds of crushed ice for a quarter. Long, heavy paper bags placed under the chute caught the ice as it was crushed.

I can remember looking through the big doors and windows of the ice plant to see how they made the ice. There were big steel vats that they used. They filled them with water from a garden hose, and when it was frozen, they turned it upside down and a huge block of ice rolled out of the vat. It had seams in it that when hit with an ice pick would break into twenty-five pound blocks.

We had a hand crank White Mountain ice cream maker. It made a good gallon at a time. We could fill it to the brim and then close the lid. Usually, we made vanilla. Around the cylinder we would fill the bucket with ice and a lot of heavy salt. We put the wooden ice cream maker in a galvanized bucket to catch the salt water that poured out of a hole in the side of the ice cream maker. The thawing of the ice is what made the metal can inside get cold which in turn froze the milk formula into ice cream. I helped turn that crank a lot, sparing my dad, because your arm sure would get tired after a few minutes. I used to watch my arm muscle seem to grow while turning the crank. You can get that cream a lot harder with the hand crank maker than with the electric machines of the modern era. It took about 25-30 minutes on a hot day to freeze the ice cream.

During the week in the summer, Mother would make homemade ice cream in the refrigerator in the big double ice tray. While it was freezing, she would take it out periodically and stir it so it wouldn't freeze so hard. She would dice this cream with sweet red cherries and fruit cocktail or sometimes we just had plain vanilla or chocolate. We would all eat the ice cream right out of the tray. I would have to say it was the best ice cream ever made, even better than the cranked kind.

11. CASTOR OIL AND CROUP

In the old days we did not have all of the modern medical remedies. A lot of the treatment was simple and home spun. We would read in our big medical journey and try to treat ourselves or go to see Doctor Joe Allison if we were really sick or he would come to see us at home. We had aspirin, milk of magnesia, and castor oil. There were warm baths and heating pads. The tools of the trade.

The caster bean, I am told, is poisonous and could kill you. Castor oil was nearly as dangerous. You knew you were in trouble when you started coughing and got what was called the croup, which caused a rattling sound in your throat and heavy breathing. You had a loud barking cough and difficulty breathing. Croup is a respiratory infection caught from air borne droplets. It causes a swelling of the inside of the trachea. It always seemed to strike at night. I remember seeing the fear in my parents' eyes, or at least the concern, when I was having trouble breathing. It was also hard to go to sleep. I remember having the croup often in the summertime for three or four years. Then I guess I outgrew it.

If given the choice, I had rather have taken a spanking than have to swallow that teaspoon filled with castor oil. My dad never took the castor oil except when he was constipated.

For other illness, like a cold, he would take a snort of whiskey straight. That was the only purpose he kept a bottle around. That remedy was not available to me, of course.

12. RUB BOARDS AND CHURNS

Every cow we ever had was a Jersey. The milk cow had to be milked twice a day even in the wintertime. This was Dad's job and I didn't accompany him to witness him milking very often because it was always before sunrise or after sunset. There was no electricity in the barn, so it was dark. Sometimes my dad would take a flashlight with him. We had one stall and it was pretty small. For some reason a milk cow always likes to kick when someone is milking her tits, so I stayed in the house most of the time so I wouldn't get kicked or be in the way of my dad. When I was there, I remember my dad made it look easy. He had a lot of experience from his days on the farms in Denton County. I found out from Dad that there is a method to milking and getting the rhythm. You have to wash the cow's tits and massage them a little bit to relax the cow so she would give the milk. Then you have to squeeze and pull a certain way to get the job done.

What I remember most was what happened next in the kitchen. Dad would bring that pale of milk in and set it in the sink. Mother would pour it into pitchers and put in the refrigerator for the cream to rise. I used to like to peak in and see how fast it was rising.

Then came the churning. We had an old white crock churn with a dasher. This job seemed to fall to Mother. It was an after-dinner job. I take it was the hardest of jobs, because it took a lot of churning to make butter. It seemed like one cow made too much for a family of four. We always had milk and butter to give away or sell at the store.

Churning was akin to the rub board. The rub board was Mother's duty too. Churning seemed to always take place on cold winter nights, and washing and rubbing always seemed to occur in the sweltering hot summertime though I know they both were year-round jobs.

Mother washed in a number two galvanized washtub. The patented rub board was made from either light weight tin or glass mounted onto a wooden frame. Mother boiled the water to get it hot and then she would pull the clothes up out of the water and rubbed them up and down the board until they were clean. I never could tell how she knew when they were finished. Next, she would rinse the clothes in clean, cold water and run them through a ringer to get the water out of the cloths so they would dry faster on the clothesline. Only a mother would know the secrets to something like that.

The washing took place every week, usually on Saturday mornings. I know Mother was glad to get that electric washer with the ringer. It set on the back porch, but she brought it in the house when she was using it. Mother still used that rub board to get all of the stains out of my pants and make sure they were clean. I guess that all of this process you would call progress because my grandmother had to wash their clothes in a big cast iron wash pot that was heated by a wood fire to get the water hot.

13. THE CELLAR AND STORMY NIGHTS

Stories of storms in the area were not soon forgotten by citizens. Tornados that blew people away and killed them and stuck chicken feathers into trees were horrifying to people as well as the grief and damage they caused. We lived in a place that was known as "Tornado Alley."

We had a cellar in the back yard near the back porch. It was made from concrete and stood up above the ground about two feet. It had a stovepipe in the center for an air hole. The door was made of wood and set on heavy hinges.

The cellar was a constant problem because it seeped water during the rainy season, which was also the storm season. We had to pump the water out with a hand pump or bucket. Dad put a coat of sealer on the walls, like a thick whitewash, which helped for a while. The cellar wasn't used to store can goods, just as protection from storms. However, I understand my grandparents used the cellar for storing vegetables, on shelves in the back of the room, when it was new.

I used to raise the door after I was strong enough, just out of curiosity, to see if there was any water, snakes or bugs inside, just like I used to pull the cover back over the fireplace to check for chimney sweeps. Sometimes I would even go in cautiously to see if it was dry. I was worried there might be a snake in there. It usually had a musty smell. There were always leaves or other debris to have to safely traverse.

We went into the cellar during bad storms. Dad would listen to the radio and know when it was time to go. We took a flashlight, lantern, and axe with us in case the big hackberry tree in the back yard fell over the door. The door had a rope tied to its side and we would have to hold on to it to keep the wind from blowing the door open. We spent some scary nights in the cellar wondering if our house was still there. We would not come out until the thunder and wind calmed down and the storm was over.

My Grandmother Tate also had a cellar at her place. She was scared to death of storms and went to the cellar often. Living in Denton County, she had seen what these storms could do to property, and she had friends who had died in tornados. The lightning itself was a significant risk that made you want to take cover. I don't know why people stopped building cellars. The houses are built stronger, but so are the storms. Instead of just plucking the chickens and sticking the feathers in the trees, the tornado just blew big oak trees down and scattered the house and its contents over the entire neighborhood.

14. CHINABERRIES AND SLING SHOTS

Our neighbors had a chinaberry tree on the corner of their property, and along the fence line on the north and halfway across the west of our garden plot, chinaberries sprouted each spring and grew faster than any plant I'd ever seen.

The trees grew straight and tall and didn't have any branches except at the very top. This made the young saplings look like Dow pins. The wood was soft and pliable. I'd look them all over and pick only the very best for making arrows and bows. I discovered that I could chop them down with a grubbing hoe or, with a little extra work, even my small pocketknife. I didn't have a hatchet until later and I didn't dare use the axe. The trees grew up in the hog wire that surrounded the garden, and after I relieved them of their roots, I would have to thread them through the wire to get them free. They also sprouted out in the garden, but those got plowed up each year and never were large enough to be used for material to build anything.

I would take a larger chinaberry sapling if I needed a new bow, but willow wood made the best bows. I usually was interested in making arrows for my quiver; it seems that arrows were easy to lose in the garden and along the fence lines. Sometimes they got hung up in the top of a tree beyond my reach. I didn't know how to attach feathers to arrow at first, though we had plenty in the barnyard. It took some study on my part. I tried to glue the feathers on, and they would stay for a while, but then fall off. I later learned in scouting that the Native Americans split the feather down the middle and then tied them on the arrow by wrapping twine around each end. I didn't know how to make arrow points either with flint and a buckhorn, so I just sharpened the end of the stick and notched the backend. In just a few minutes I had a new arrow to shoot. I tried to make arrow points by chiseling them out of the top of a tin can, with a hammer and a ten-penny nail, but they were too soft and bent on impact. Some arrows would be better than others. Some would shoot straight, and others would wobble. I kept the good ones and didn't waste my time with the ones that were imperfect. It took my breath to watch the flight of the arrow. Every time I shot one it looked in flight like it would hit its target, but so many times there was a limb that I hadn't seen or some other object that would deflect the flight of the arrow. Hunting with a bow and arrow took a lot of practice and a lot of skill.

My dad made me a sling shot out of the fork of a limb and attached rubber bands made from an old tire inner tube that he got at Willhoites Garage. I used small rocks from the yard to shoot my prey. In season I used the chinaberries. They were smooth and round and hard before they got too ripe. They made good ammunition for the slingshot. Of course, they were not a deadly weapon but were fun to shoot. I frightened a lot of songbirds that way before they became protected.

I shot the chinaberries in the air just to see how high they would go, much like I did my arrows. There wasn't any game in the yard except a few sparrows and maybe a blue jay or mockingbird. I knew not to shoot at the mockingbirds because they were sacred. This left the sparrow as my main target, but I don't think I ever killed or wounded one. I did get a lot of shots and that was where the fun came in.

I made knives out of wood. I carved a hunting knife and made me a scabbard just like my dad had, except I made mine out of bark from the old crepe myrtle tree and sewed it together with a thread. We had a berry tree in the front of the house that had two-inch long thorns that you could break off to use as a needle. I knew better than to get in my mother's sewing basket or I would have gotten in the worst of trouble. One of the first principles to learn growing up was to " know where your limits are."

A handy man that hung out at the hardware store showed me how to make a bird trap out of a tomato crate and three small sticks that made the shape of the number 4. The three small sticks were notched. One held the box up, one was longer and extended under the box. This was the trigger. When a bird hit it or jumped up on it, the box would fall and the bird was trapped. The other one extended from trigger stick to the top of the stick holding the box up. When the trigger was hit, the sticks all collapsed like dominos, bringing the box down around its innocent victim. We put chicken feed under the box to bait it. I always released anything I caught, but it was a lot of fun.

William D. Tate

15. THE CAT CARRIED IT OFF

There was a feral cat that had taken up residency with us. It had just wandered in, and I fed it and of course it stayed. It was a solid white cat that we called Snowball. It was always around our feet purring, and it became a good friend and my alibi. There was a special brick that the family used for the purpose of propping closed the side gate to the yard. It was a large brick, orange in color, and had a five-point star embedded in the center. Then one day the brick disappeared. My mother asked me what I had done with the brick. I felt like I had been unfairly profiled because there was no evidence that led to me. There were other neighbor children that had being playing in our yard. I don't know whether I did not remember or whether I was trying to avoid getting in trouble. At any rate, I said on a lark, "I don't know, I guess the cat carried it off." It was a legitimate argument to me, and it seemed to satisfy my mother at the time. I am sure she thought this was a prank or wisecrack, but she didn't say that to me. As I grew up the "cat carried it off" became a family joke. My mother told all the family and they mocked me about the "cat carrying it off." When something of mine disappeared, and I asked my mom or dad if they knew what happened to it, they would say, "No, I guess the cat carried it off." So I paid the price for my indiscretion.

Footnote: My daughter Sheri and her husband Chad own the house where I grew up, the fourth generation to live there. While writing this book, my son-in-law was replacing the teardrop siding on the outside of the dinning room, about fifteen feet from the gate that the brick used to keep closed. The next day I was by there and Sheri showed me a brick that Chad had found under the house. I noticed immediately the perfect five-pointed star in the center of the brick and I said, "Oh, that is the brick that the cat carried off." She said, "He found it under the house." I thought about the brick the next day and it all came back to me in a flashback. I could see myself in action and what I had done with the brick. I noticed, that day, that an animal had dug a hole underneath the house. My worst fear when I was exploring under the house was that I would run into an unexpected snake or varmint. To protect myself against that, I decided to fill the hole up so such a creature could not enter through the hole. There was not enough dirt to fill up the hole, so I put the brick in the hole and covered it up with dirt. I asked Chad later where under the house that he found the brick and he said, "Right under the wall that I took down and it was partially covered in dirt." For seventy years I had forgotten what I had done with the brick, and even though I had been improperly accused. I didn't realize it was such an important brick, and if I could have remembered at the time my mother confronted me about it, I'm sure I would have just dug the brick up and returned it to its proper place against the gate.

16. CHURCH AND SUNDAY SCHOOL

My mother's family had been members of the Methodist Church for several generations. My Grandfather Bennett had been Sunday school superintendent. We only lived a block away from the church building so we walked to church on Church Street. Large steps led to the upstairs sanctuary and steps down into the basement where Sunday school was held. There was a bell tower in the northwest corner of the building with a large bell and a rope to ring it. There were several vitex trees along the front where the cars were parked. There were chairs in the back for the choir to set. In the sanctuary was a large pulpit made of walnut that had been built and donated to the church by my mother's family in memory of their loved ones. The Leach Hall, made to look like a log cabin, was on the north side of the church, next to the parsonage, where the preacher lived. It was a large two story, white frame house that sat on the corner with a large porch swing on the front porch.

My mother always wanted me to go to Sunday school, which I admit was more interesting than church itself. We colored pictures of biblical events and talked about passages from the Bible, depending on the time of year. The basement was either cold or hot. The walls were concrete. There were several classrooms down there and a kitchen for events. After Sunday school we climbed the interior stairs up to the sanctuary. When I was a kid, I would set with my parents. We also went on Sunday night and I remember the ceiling fans that tried desperately to make the room temperature bearable with little success. Attendees would supplement with hand, held cardboard advertising fans to add to the circulation. I would crawl around the wooden floor under the pews and legs and feet to entertain myself and squelch my boredom. We also had a revival every summer, which meant we had to go every night. When I started the sixth grade, I could go to the balcony and sit with the other young people. This made church more appealing. I would read marriage ceremonies from the hymnal and pretend that I was marrying some pretty girl. When you reached the balcony, you had arrived and were in the "in" group. Sunday became an event, and I did not mind going to church anymore.

17. SETTING HENS AND BANTAMS

There was nothing more challenging and daring to a small boy than going into hen houses, checking on setting hens and varmints. Mother taught me how to hold their heads back with a stick to get their eggs or to see if they had hatched.

I usually didn't have a stick, and I thought that was a little "sissy" so I usually just used my hand, unless it was a real rough hen. I didn't bother the eggs. It was a lot of fun to count the eggs. We had a white painted hen house in the barnyard. It had a small door on the east side for the hens to come and go. The entrance door was on the west. The front had an opening about three and half feet off the ground and across the width of the house for ventilation. It was covered in one-inch chicken wire.

Inside had a frame with runners and cross bars hanging from the ceiling for the chickens to roost. This kept them high off the ground to keep varmints, like possums, from getting them at night. The nests were in boxes nailed to the side of the walls. The walls were painted with creosote from time to time, so the chicken house had a petroleum odor that offset the natural odors. You had to be very careful not to brush up against the walls or you would get that black tar looking creosote on your clothes. This creosote process was necessary to keep the mites away.

Dad would go in and clean the manure out of the hen house every spring and spread the fertilizer on the garden. I remember him telling me that if you could got too much chicken manure on a plant it would burn it up.

We usually had a mixture of chickens. Sometimes my dad would go buy some young pullets and bring them home. Dad would tie their legs together with binder twine and put them in a burlap potato sack to carry them home. Because I like chickens, Dad got me some bantams. I had my choice and I picked out some Buff Orpingtons with feathers on their legs, because my grandparents always raised Buff Orpington chickens each year. We purchased a trio of the bantams and raised a few little ones. We ate the roosters and kept the pullets.

A few times I talked Dad into stopping and buying me a dozen chicks, but more times than not he would turn me down because we could hatch our own baby chicks. The hens often clucked just after they laid their egg. The clucking of a hen was a familiar sound throughout the neighborhood, and in the early morning hours the crowing of roosters were sounds to be remembered.

It was interesting that everyone had their favorite breed of chickens and stayed with the breed. Ed and Belle McCombs, who lived in a house on the north side of Franklin Street, always had White Leghorns. Some thought they were the best layers of white eggs. Jody and Sue Lipscomb to our east had White Rocks. Mr. Hart, down the street, had Plymouth Rocks; I used to visit these hen houses often just to check them out and see what they had that we didn't.

Back then eggs were not regulated by the state or federal government, and people raised extra eggs to sell. They would sell them to individual customers or take them to town to sell at the grocery stores for cash or exchange for groceries. Nearly all of the eggs were fertile and if they were not fresh the embryo would start to grow. I used to watch employees of the grocery store candle the eggs brought in to make sure they were fresh, clear, and eatable. The candling process was the placing of an egg in a small hole in a cardboard box with a light inside, that allowed you to see inside the egg.

My dad went to South Dakota pheasant hunting each fall. He started raising pheasants, so he built a large wire pen on the east side of the garage. It had the old, v-roofed doghouse inside for shelter. We had pheasants there for several years, but he had to tear it down when the garage had to be extended. We would collect the eggs off the ground each day. When we got enough, we would set the pheasant eggs under bantam hens. When the eggs would hatch, we would let the baby chicks have the run of the backyard for a few days. To get them started on a high protein diet, Mother would boil chicken eggs and we would carve them up with a dinner knife. They sure loved boiled eggs.

18. BEDROLLS & PAINTED NAILS:

Every fall when I was a kid, my father would get ready for the opening day of deer season. He hunted on the James River Ranch in Kimbell County, Texas with Jess Hall and other locals. We often took a vacation in the summer to Mason in the Texas Hill County, and I couldn't wait until I got big enough to go hunting with my dad in the fall. He had a brown sleeping bag made of tarp cloth that had a small mattress inside. He kept it stored in the off season on the balcony at the grocery store. He would bring it home and spread it out in the dining room, so Mother could add sheets and some blankets for the trip. My dad then rolled it up as tight as he could. He had some 2 1/2-inch web bands with big buckles that he wrapped around the bed roll to keep it as tight as possible so it could be picked up and carried.

The window seat in the dining room is where his long handles, tan moleskin pants, and wool hunting shirts were kept when not in use. These were pulled out and tried on to see if they still fit and then placed them in a black cardboard barrel with rope handles. This was the beginning of the ritual. Then my mother would paint my dad's toenails with bright, red fingernail polish, which he believed would bring him good luck while hunting. It must have worked because my dad always seemed to get his two buck deer every year. When Dad left for a few days, Mother and I would stay at my Grandmother Tate's house until he returned. My granddad also went deer hunting, on another lease than my dad, so he was gone too. It was a mutual arrangement to give my grandmother and us company and to make sure each was provided for. After the hunt the ritual was reversed, the clothes and sheets washed and put away for another year.

One year my dad got back from the deer hunt late at night. The next morning, he had a surprise for me in a tow sack. There was something alive in the sack. He had me feel of the sack and try to guess what kind of creature was there. I could tell it wasn't a deer or a dog or anything like that. I gave up. We opened the sack and it was an armadillo. I had never seen one before. It looked like a small dinosaur with a hard shell back, sharp nose, and a long scaly tail. They were plentiful in the deer country, and my dad had slipped up on one and caught it and brought it home for a pet. We put it in a pen, but it soon got out and disappeared. We never saw it again. Other hunters must have done the same thing because it wasn't many years until armadillos were found around town digging in flower beds and causing mischief.

19. SHOE SHOPPING AND RUDE AWAKENINGS:

We went to Ft. Worth shopping for shoes and clothes a couple of times a year. We would park in Leonard Bros. parking garage. I can remember that in the lobby entering the store there were separate rest rooms and water fountains for whites and colored people. I had never seen this before and it confused me. We did not have such separation in Grapevine, but we did have segregated schools at the time. The members of the African American community were welcome to use the facilities in our stores and some did. African Americans were some of our best customers and my good friends. Bill Jordan, who worked on the Crabtree Ranch on State Highway 121, rode his big strawberry roam horse to town. His hands were knotty from the arthritis and his legs bow-legged from too many days on a horse. I was always glad to see him because he had interesting stories to tell. He was the last Grapevine cowboy to ride his horse to town. There was Rev. Pete Redmon, who worked for B & D Mills during the week. I would see him pass our house at dusk during the week, covered with mill dust. He was also, a gospel preacher at Love Chapel Church. Then there was Walter McKenzie, who reminded me of Uncle Remus. His hands were as big as sledge-hammers and his feet even bigger. He worked on the construction of the Grapevine Dam and then retired and stayed here. He, like my great-grandmother, was illiterate. He would come into the grocery store to cash his Social Security check because he had to endorse it with an X and have it witnessed. We would guarantee his signature. We delivered groceries to African American families. I looked up to these men and other men and women like them that lived in our community.

While in Ft. Worth we went to places like Striplings, Leonard Bros, Monning's, and the Red Goose shoe store. The shoe store had a lot of shoes in the window, so you could see if they had anything you liked before you went in and tried them on. You were lucky if they had in your size the kind of shoe that you liked as a child. My parents made the final choice, based on price, looks, and durability. We would look at the shoes in the store windows and then go in. A salesman would come by and measure my foot with a metal contraption. You put your foot on metal plate, then the clerk would move a sliding metal piece to the point of your toe. The device would calculation the shoe size that was appropriate for a person's feet, including width as well as length. My mother was always curious to see how much my feet had grown since the last time we bought shoes. I would try the shoes on, then the clerk would pinch the end of the shoe to see where my toes were and ask me how they felt. They always felt better in the store than they did later breaking them in.

As I got older, we went shopping less and less into Ft. Worth, and made our purchases instead at home. E.J. Lipscomb and Son had a dry goods store next to our hardware store, and they too had shoes displayed in the windows but not nearly as many to choose from as the Red Goose shoe store. Lipscomb's Dry Goods did not always have shoes I liked in my size. Mr. Huber Lipscomb, who was the owner of the store, would try to sell me anything in my size that he had in stock. It seemed that the ugliest pair of shoes he had in the store was the one size that would fit my feet. I had no choice but to buy them if I needed a new pair of shoes. I usually went barefooted from the first day of the summer school recess until school started again in September. The end of summer is when I usually got to buy a new pair of shoes. My mother made my shirts until I reached junior high. My homemade shirts and ugly shoes made me feel very self-conscious about my looks and gave me an inferiority complex. I hoped someday to get over it.

20. DOMINO GAMES AND SMOKE:

Nearly everyone liked to play 42 or dominos back when I was a child. There were domino halls and pool parlors located on Main Street. Mostly people played with friends in someone's home on what they called "card tables" which were square folding tables with four sides. Some played a game called "checkers" over at Abbie Statum's Gulf Station.

After the war when my uncles came home from the service, and the family was together again, they would gather on a Friday or Saturday night at my grandparents' house on Wall Street and pay dominos and 42 into the late hours. For the players it was a romp, a caper that to some extent became a crusade. I never was so bored in my life. It was all I could do to stay up. There was nothing for the kids to do even though the house was full of kids. It was too dark to go outside and play. We had to be quiet and not make a peep. This was before television. Dominos is a game of concentration. My grandfather smoked Camel cigarettes, and my uncles Erman and Clois came home from the war smoking cigarettes too. The room was always filled with so much smoke you could hardly breathe. It is a wonder we didn't get some respiratory disease. My father didn't smoke. Instead, he chewed Tinsley or Beechnut tobacco. My grandmother dipped snuff, so there was not only the smoke but the spitting too. There was a lot of hollering, talking, boasting, bragging, laughing, and clinking of dominions. I don't know what advantage it gave the player to knocking the dominos together or thumping them on the table. In the end the best player almost always won. After every game there had to be a review of the game, who played what and why, what mistakes were made, and what the strategy was that led to victory. They almost never took a break for a drink of water, coffee, or anything, including going to the bathroom. The games were just too intense. We kids usually fell asleep on the chairs, beds, couch, and floors wherever we could find a place. We knew better to ask any questions or to say anything especially refraining from asking the question, "When are we going home?"

21. PECAN TREES AND OTHER FRUITS

The old, stately native pecan tree stood for decades at the edge of the garden. It was there when my grandparents moved their house on the north lot on Church Street and built their new house facing College Street. It was on the fence line, so half the pecans fell on Dollie and Mr. Charlie's side of the fence, the other half on our garden. The fence line really didn't make any difference to me. I worked both sides. In fact, there was a hole in the hog wire fence next to the tree, which was one of my regular paths through the neighborhood. It was a like a river crossing.

I always watched to make sure that the majestic tree put out new leaves in the spring.

We never sprayed for worms or anything and never pruned the tree, except when the wind or ice broke off a limb or two. I am not sure why I liked that old tree so much, except for the nuts it produced in the fall. The pecans were usually small, but these native ones were all you could find back then. The budding and grafting of paper shell pecans would come later.

A few pecans fell each year while they were still covered in their green shell. I would peal the green wrapper and get my hands and clothes stained green by the juice. It didn't come off very easily either. I could always tell my mother's displeasure, when she saw the pecan stains on my clothes. But she liked for me to pick up the good pecans for her to shell and cook with, so she never was too hard on me when I got a little dirty in the process.

I would get a stick and knock the lower nuts off the tree or jump and pull the branches that were in my reach down or try to knock the pecans out with clods from the garden or with my slingshot. This was a tradition that occurred year after year, until one year the tree went to sleep and never woke up. It was the end of an era and an emotional point in my life. I still have a special interest in pecan trees.

We had another pecan tree that sprouted in the yard, and Dr. Rodney Shelton, a vocational agricultural teacher, tried to bud it with a paper shell variety, but it didn't work. I watched him do it. It was very interesting. He took a double-bladed knife and cut a strip of bark about three-fourths of an inch wide and three inches long from an area that had a limb budding. He then placed a similar piece of bark and bud from another tree over the removed area. He then sealed and wrapped the area of incision on the tree. Unfortunately, the buds did not take and died.

While I am talking about trees, I had another favorite tree. It was a sycamore tree that stood in the front yard of Ernest Lowe's house across College Street from our house. It had those great big leaves and white bark. When the leaves fell in the fall they ended up in our yard. The leaves were shaped like a hand but were even bigger than mine. Some of the bark peeled off the tree and would also end up in our yard. I lost this tree too, the year after the old pecan tree died. I always vowed that I would plant such a tree in my yard someday.

My Tate grandparents had an orchard of peach, pear, and plum trees. They had a large yellow plum tree just behind their house that always made a lot of fruit. It was good to eat them right off the tree. Mother also made plum preserves each year with the seed and plum skin left in the preserves. My grandparents also had blackberry bushes around their house. I liked to pick them off the vine and eat them, though they were also good with cereal or in a cobbler. The berries always stained my hands, and the thorns scared my arms for days, but it was a worthy venture. They also had one of those big native pecan trees in the back yard like so many other families.

We planted a row of fruit trees along the edge of our garden one year. They never did too well. The yellow plum produced for a few years and then died. The peach trees were also short-lived and produced little fruit. The Bartlett pear tree lived the longest but never did make real good fruit. We tried replanting the trees after several years but finally gave up. The fruit trees did better in the sandy soil like my Granddad Tate had in his garden, compared to the black soil that we had at home. Picking plums and peaches off the tree to eat and letting the juice run down your arm is the best way to enjoy different kinds of summer fruit.

22. THE GARAGE

The old garage had been built years before my time for smaller cars. It sat near Church Street on the west side of our property. There was a culvert and a gravel approach. The garage was made from foot wide yellow pine with a three-inch bat to cover the crack where the boards met. It was originally painted white, but I don't think it was ever repainted. Many of the garages and outbuildings in the neighborhood were never painted at all but had a natural weathered look. The garage had the same green shingles to match the house, two large doors that swung open to either side, and a chain that held them together. When the chain lock was left opened, I often entered to explore and play and just see what you might find in such a place. The rafters were used to store things and the floor was gravel.

When the cars got larger, Dad had Uncle Arthur Tate to add a thirty-inch extension on the east end, high enough for the hood to slip under and for the garage doors to close. It was still a tight squeeze.

The garage had a particular odor that all outbuildings had—that kind of musty smell you never forget. It had a gravel floor. There was no light in the garage so when we came in after dark, we had to make our way to the house out of habit, experience, and intuition, and hope that there were no surprises waiting in the bushes.

There was of course storage in the garage. Boxes and boards sat on the rafters. There were shelves at the east end of the garage where odds and ends were kept, including old cans of paint, oil, and poisons. It is where the old wooden telephone set for years after it was replaced by the black plastic phones that represented a new generation of telephones. These new telephones replaced the wall telephones across the country as well as our local telephone operator that we called "Central."

The garage was a familiar playground. I liked to go in and sit in the car and play with the steering wheel and other knobs and things, and pretend I was driving. I also explored through the storage. It was challenging because I knew I wasn't supposed to be in there. The garage housed only the car. For some reason the pickup was always parked in the backyard.

There was a Crepe Myrtle tree that grew at the end of the garage on the opposite side from the garden. A hackberry tree grew on the northwest corner that allowed access to the roof. The roof was very steep, and I was reluctant to leave the tree for the roof. I had easier targets and access to roofs and I always practiced safety first. That is why I never ended up with a broken arm or leg.

23. THE BARN

A tin barn sat at the back of the property in the barnyard. It had a small stall on one end with a slatted wooden door for ventilation. The stall had a dirt floor. It was where a calf was stabled or a cow milked. The barn had a wooden floor, except the stall. There was one window in the barn with a tin door that would cover the window when raised and latched. It was tin like the rest of the barn, but often the window that was hinged on the bottom would be open. I could jump on the window frame and lift myself in through the window, twas the way I like to enter the barn.

The barn was another interesting venue, like all the out builds, each unique unto itself.

Inside we stored feed for the chickens, cow and sometimes a pig. It is also were we kept our tools and there where two big wooden boxes in which we kept old toys, pictures, and family stuff because we didn't have enough closet space in the house.

I guess because of the accessibility and the feed, every once in a while, the rats would take over. I would go out at night with my dad and hold the flashlight while he would shoot the rats with a 22 shot as they ran along the rafters just under the roof.

My Uncle Dick gave us a female Irish setter hunting dog that had two litters of pups in the barn. They were crossed with an English pointer called Rex. They were either solid brown or black but not good for hunting, because they neither set nor pointed. We gave them all away.

Later the barn was moved closer to the hen house when my mother and her sister divided up their parents' property. It is the only out buildings that survived the modernization period when the hen house and out house were moved to our farm in the country.

My dad had a steer in the lot and had put up a heavy telephone wire to keep the steer away from the barn. My cousin Lanny Tate and I were playing in the lot one day and decided to run for the barn. We forgot about the wire and it caught us both at the same time under the neck and caused us to take a double flip. We could not imagine what had hit us until we looked up and saw the wire and felt the scratch it put on our necks. We tied some cloth to the wire after that to keep from making the same mistake twice.

The barn is where I had my incubator. The incubator had six trays holding six hundred eggs encased in a red wood cabinet. I was very proud to have such a fine machine. It was the successor to a fifty-egg, round, metal incubator that I first started hatching quail and pheasant eggs. We had tried to keep the incubator in the cellar because of the moisture, but the seepage made me decide to move it to the barn. It was a perfect place. I liked to hatch chickens and quails. The quail were a hobby. The chickens were one of my businesses. The chickens I hatched were cross breeds. Dad sold the chicks in the store and gave me the money. It was my first business venture for personal profit and provided me with some spending money. A kid needed capital to exercise all of his vast freedoms.

24. MUD PIES AND SPRINKLERS

Dad had a truck load of play sand hauled in and dumped in the back yard. It made a good mixer with the hard, black loam for making mud pies. This was one of the few activities that the boys and girls could do together though I don't remember my sister spending much time cooking with mud.

We would take an old tin can, fill it with the right amount of soil, and add a spice of leaves, bugs, or grass depending on what was in season, then stir with a stick until properly mixed. We would pour the batter out on a board like pancakes or if available a small pan for cakes and cookies. Then we would let it bake in the sun, at the right temperature, until hard, where you knew it was done. The fun, of course, was in the imagination because we never sampled even the best of recipes.

As each summer arrived, it was hard to find a cool spot during the day. The windows in the house were opened and the fans full speed, but everyone was interested in water. We didn't have a swimming pool in those days, unless we went to Sylvania Park on Belknap Street in Fort Worth. So we improvised.

The end of the clothesline was made out of a large square, wooden post. We connected the round, tubular water sprinkle that we used on the yard to the water hose. Then we tied the water sprinkler to the top of the clothesline post. We stood on a large platform made of wood that Dad had made as a speaker's stand when ground was broken for the Grapevine Dam. In the middle of the day, we would get in our bathing suits, turn on the water, and cool off. It made a mud hole for the farm animals to drink or cool off as well. Sometimes when we had extra eggs, I would collect a couple from the hen house and break them open and fry them on the sidewalk in the August heat. We knew they were not good to eat because we did not have any salt or pepper to put on them. It was just for play. I never really learned to swim.

25. PICKET FENCES AND TRAILS:

The town was filled with picket fences. The fences were there for decoration but also to hold in chickens or a cow, or in some cases to keep livestock out of the gardens. Take Mr. Charlie Berry my neighbor, for example. He had two separate garden spots surrounded on three sides by unpainted picket fences. There was a time when he raised some bronze turkeys for Thanksgiving and Christmas. He also had some chickens, but no livestock. For the most part the fences were used to plant climbing butter beans and green beans on like a trellis. He would take string and run it from the top of the picket to the ground for the plants to grow and run on.

Our yard had picket fences beginning at the back door to the west and then along Church Street to the garage, from the back of the house east forming a large barnyard and a smaller pen on the front. My grandfather had built it out of beaded ceiling. I walked the picket fences a lot. Each trip was a vagary or unpredictable and unusual journey. The fences were leaning in places, and there were gates to negotiate and other hurdles. It was a challenge to see how far I could travel through town on the picket fences without falling off.

I had certain paths that I created through the neighborhood. These were not game trails or old Indian trails; they were trails establish by my patterns. There was a gate next to the Berry's car shed, but I preferred going through a hole in the fence at the old pecan tree or climbing over the shed for entry. I visited Charlie and Dollie a lot and explored their property on a daily basis. I had a path from our back door through our garden, which let to the wire fence. I would then wind through the flower beds to their backyard.

A second path took me down the picket fence on the west side of our barnyard to the Berry shed, which path took me on top of the shed for a lookout, then down the wire fence into the Berry's garden, through the garden gate into their backyard or on to Franklin Street on the way to my father's store.

I also established a more substantial trail in the front yard, using hoe and shovel to make a bicycle trail complete with speed bumps and other obstacles. My sister and I would take turns riding our bicycles around and around this course. There were five large hackberry trees along the sidewalk in the front yard so there was not much grass under the trees to disturb. We made these crude improvements as an obstacle course and had fun both in construction and performances.

26. GARDENS AND EARTHWORMS

I remember being awakened early on Saturday mornings in early spring or fall to hear the sound of Miley Woodall or Sam Thompson shouting out instructions to their horse or mule as they began plowing the garden in the backyard. "Whoa, girl, back up to the plow." Miley had a small square trailer that just set up off the ground on metal wheels in which he carried his plow and other equipment. Miley had a mule and Sam an iron colored mare.

Dad knew to wait until there was enough moisture in the ground that the field would not break into hard clods but would easily harrow. I was amazed at how deep the plow cut into the ground. I enjoyed the smell of fresh plowed ground, so I always jumped out of bed and into my clothes and out to the garden.

I liked to follow the plow and watch the plowman with the leather straps over his shoulder. It was amazing how he was able to talk and guide the animal to do what he wanted him to do. He would then run the harrow over the garden to break the clods so it could be cultivated. Robins and other birds would run along behind the plow looking for something good to eat like a worm or insect.

It didn't take long to plow our garden, but there was always another garden next door that needed plowing so they just moved on. My dad was one of the few in our neighborhood that planted a fall garden. Most were through when the harvest was over at the end of summer, and everything had been burnt brown and crisp by the bitter August heat.

I liked to walk in the dirt barefoot and feel it pass between my toes like silk, as I looked for horny toads scuttling across the top of the ground after being evicted from their winter home. There were usually bounties of earth worms that were displaced and who hurried to slip back in their holes or burrow new ones. I like to pull them out of the ground or a clod and often put them in a coffee can in hopes that I could persuade my dad to take me fishing. There was a method you had to follow to get the earth worms out of the soil. If you pulled too hard then you would pull the worm in two. I was under the impression when that happened that it did not kill the worm, but made two worms instead. I didn't like to break the worms up so I learned to pull gently and then release, pull and release, and the earth worm would relax and then you could pull him on out in one piece.

Dad would lay off the rows by a push plow. He never set a string, just always eyeballed it to get the rows straight. We started the garden with onions, English peas and potatoes in the spring. The soil was black so that meant white potatoes. The red potatoes did better in the sandy soils. February 14 was planting day. The freezes were not always over, but by the time the seed sprouted, the plants seldom got frozen out. We also planted Golden Bantam sweet corn and Burpee green bush beans. We didn't plant black-eyed peas and okra until April. Sometime in between we planted Henderson bush butterbeans, and sometimes green bean or butter bean climbers on the picket fences. When Mr. Jess Hall went go to the Texas Valley to get tomato plants for his commercial operations, he always got some extras that we sold in the store. We planted our tomatoes usually in late March. Sometimes we still had to cover them if the temperature dropped below freezing. They made good tomatoes and had a lot of acid in them. After the Porter tomato was patented, we started planting those because even though the fruit was small, they made until frost.

Dad would hoe and plow in evenings after work and on Sunday after church. Mother did the gathering of beans and black eyes. We usually had plenty to pick, sometimes filling a number two washtub. Then Mother would start snapping or shelling and canned for days in pint size Mason or Kerr jars.

In the fall my dad took some of the seed that had not sold at the store like mustard, turnip greens, lettuce, spinach, radishes and Swiss chard, and mix them together, then broadcast them across the garden. When the plants were mature, neighbors and friends would come by and pick a mess for free in a brown grocery bag that we provided. Mother always picked a mess for us every couple of weeks, washed them, made sure there were no bugs on them and then cooked them to serve with pinto beans, pork, and corn bread. Vegetables from our garden were good eating not only in season but throughout the year. You could not raise watermelons or cantaloupes in the black soils so we didn't try. My parents' generation had lived through the Great Depression and the soup lines; the Dust Bowl, where thousands of animals were emaciated and people were famishing; and WWII when staple goods, like sugar and coffee, were rationed. They didn't want to be caught without enough food to eat. People just didn't have confidence in the food chain because of prior events. Gardening was hard work, but nearly every homesteader had a garden, and they went through the same rituals from season to season.

27. BROOMS AND BELTS

I grew up in the generation that believed if you spared the rod you spoiled the child, though I did not get many spankings. I was a free roamer, a free spirit, and my parents were willing to let me be what I wanted to be. My theme song could have been like the Jody Miller song "Home of the Brave": "Why won't you let me be what I want to be, I am just a little bit different." Crime was very limited at that time. Citizens did not lock their doors, and I was free to go and come into my neighbors houses and outhouses at will without complains or repercussions. I made the most of it, and this turned into a big part of my life, since I did not have a lot of playmates and had to entertain myself most of the time.

My mother was a short lady, kind and forgiving. She always wished she was taller so she could reach the top of the cabinets. When she got down on her knees, she had to pull herself up. One day I did something Mother did not like. I don't recall the details of the specific crime, but I remember the confrontation with my mother. She had apparently given out several warnings and her patience had run thin. She was going to give me a hand spanking if she could catch me, but I ran and got under the big four poster bed in the back room where I knew she couldn't get to me. She knew that too, so she got her broom and tried to poke me out, but the broom was not long enough. After she realized this method was going to fail, she made the ultimate threat. She threatened to call my dad at the store and get him to come home and spank me with his belt. Having heard this threat, when the coast was clear, I ran away to the store in hope of sanctuary with my father.

After my mother gave up, I left without telling anyone, so you might say I was a runaway. My father only spanked me one time with a belt and he did so with some anger. I did not want to experience that again. I think the spanking hurt my dad more than it did me. I was about six years of age at the time and instead of sending me home, he put me to work stocking groceries and cleaning displays in the store. It was the beginning of a new career. My mother never tried to poke me out from under he bed or spank me again.

I had pulled it off one last time.

28. STOCKING SHELVES AND INVENTORIES

When I left the house for my father's store, I cut through the path that took me through the garden, over the shed, through the Berry's yard to Franklin Street, then around the end of the McCombs corn patch to Barton Street and the back of the grocery store. I could see my father and grandfather's truck and car there so I knew I would be safe. Of course, my mother would call my father a couple of hours later to report me missing.

My dad put me to work stocking groceries. It was a boring and never-ending job. Hard work makes you grow up rather quickly. It was a milestone along the path of life for me, and I repeated this trip hundreds of times in the years that followed, but usually with my mother's permission.

Jimmy Hudgins, who worked at the store, showed me how I should dust the shelf first with a turkey feather duster. I took the older cans off the shelf and put the fresh ones in the back, then restocked the older ones in the front so they would sell first. Some of the shelves were too high for me, so I had to stand on a box of groceries or a chair to reach them. My career started in the area of the store where we stocked the Vienna sausage, Spam, and potted meat, all next to the large walnut case where the bulk beans, brown and white sugar were stored with the soaps and detergents above. Stocking groceries was a constant ritual. Dusting was an endless task, because the automobile traffic on Main Street stirred up the dust and sent it sailing in all of the businesses. I guess it was here, in my father's store, that I got my inspiration for bigger and greater things.

The first day after Christmas each year we had to start taking inventory. We had to count and price every item in the store to prepare a total of goods on hand to know how to file an income tax return. It is here that I improved my math, counting out the cans while another employee wrote down a description of the item, the number, and its value. We had a code marked on the can in letters that told us the cost. The retail price was also marked on the top of each can. This marking was done by a black or red crayon pencil. To sharpen the pencil, you pulled a string and it peeled off part of the paper around the crayon and exported more of the color. It was called a felt pen.

This inventory process went on for days. The store looked better than it did the rest of the year, because everything was clean and in its proper place. My dad would total each page to get the inventory. This was a dreaded process that was made easier for everyone only because it followed Christmas, and for me, because of all of the new toys that I had received. In the end we knew how much money the family had made the year before and whether the store inventory of goods was increasing or decreasing. It was a measuring stick.

29. DOLLIE BERRY AND MR. CHARLIE:

Our neighbors to the north were Charlie and Dollie Berry. They lived in a white frame house that used to be my mother's parents' house where she was born. The house sat on the corner, with a large front porch. The ceilings were high, the floors hardwood and often uneven. Two oval pictures of Mr. Berry's parents hung in the bedroom from long leather cords that were mounted several feet above them. Their yard was filled each year with annual flowers like poppy, larkspur, holly hawk, periwinkles, and zinnias. It was more of an enterprise than a hobby. It cut back on the mowing that had to be accomplished by a push mower. The Berrys, as did my father, had a large garden each spring and canned the surplus, and stored the vegetables in a storeroom next to the hen house and the garage. They were all built together as one building and were void of any paint. I used to climb up on top of these structures as a part of my exploration.

Ms. Dollie was small in stature and white headed. She always wore an apron, and when she went outside to work, she wore a bonnet. We engaged in a lot of chitter-chatter. I remember her hands were hardened and calloused by years of hard work. She was a good cook and was always working in the yard or the kitchen. I came and went into their house at my pleasure. If I was there at lunch time, she always asked me if I wanted to stay and eat and I would al-

My Barefoot Days

ways say, " I guess so," especially if she had what I liked, such as fried chicken, black-eyed peas, cabbage, or corn on the cob.

I remember Mr. Charlie raised a good garden and kept it free of weeds. He was industrious about his garden. He always planted cabbage. I like to see it grow, because it grew really fast. He planted climbing green beans and butter beans on the picket fences around their garden on white cotton cord he'd strung for them to run on.

He liked to sit on the back porch and whittle. He was also a small person. To me he was like another grandfather. He took everything seriously and had a dogmatic and somber personality. He talked with me a lot and taught me a lot about the good and honest things in life. He was also a good carpenter and made furniture for their house and perhaps other families. He taught me how to sharpen a hoe and put a new handle on a shovel. Mr. Charlie probed and scrutinized everything and knew how to do almost everything.

They never had a milk cow or a hog like we did, but they did raise white leghorn chickens each year. The chickens were free roaming during the day and were cooped up in the hen house at night to keep Mr. Possum from cutting their necks in two. One year, Mr. Charlie got some turkey eggs from Mr. Jim Davis who raised bronze turkeys west of town. The eggs were placed under a setting hen and hatched. That was the only year he raised turkeys, a one-year initiative. My dad bought one for Thanksgiving, and I have very vivid memories about how the turkey hen came to die and how she was bathed in boiling water to loosen the feathers. I participated in this chore and was impressed with the length of time and effort it took to clean the turkey. It was hard to pull the tail and wing feathers out of the bird. You could not buy turkeys in the grocery stores back then so if you were one of the lucky ones that had a turkey for Thanksgiving or Christmas, you had to raise your own or buy one from a nearby farm. We usually just had an old laying hen instead that served our small family.

I have fond members of the Christmas seasons at Ms. Berry's house. She always had a small tree that set on a coffee table. The wrappings of paper and ribbons were all about the house. There were always a lot of Christmas cards to be sent and a lot received. The house was always filled with a good aroma from the kitchen where Christmas candies, cakes, and pies were prepared. A back door to the house allowed entry to the restroom, and I visited these facilities more than I did my own. The house had a lot of windows so I could see what was going on inside while playing in the yard.

Mr. Charlie and Dolly had four children, three boys and a girl: Ray, Sandy Willis, J. E. and, Corrine. Willis had a daughter named Beverly and a son named Sandy. They came to visit their grandparents often on the weekends.

I remember when Mr. Charlie got sick and was on his death bed. I was told that he had asthma. He was the first person I knew who died. The only thing I understood about death was that I didn't like it. They brought his body back to the house and he lay in state where the Christmas tree always stood. Men sat up with Mr. Charlie that last night in the house.

30 ATTICS AND THOSE SORT OF THINGS.

I was an explorer at a very young age, with a huge curiosity that had to be pleased anyway possible. I considered it was my duty to seek out each and every possibility for discovery. Of course, every house has an attic. In the beginning we had a small hole in the ceiling in the kitchen where Dad could go up to check the wiring and the roof. Then we had a pull-down ladder installed in the hallway so the attic could be used for more things, including storage. It was an adventure in the making. An opportunity to see how the house was built. There was a chimney in the living room, but also a smaller one in the kitchen that went through the roof. It had been used when meals were cooked on a wood stove, but long since had been sealed off. You could see the wiring and the roof. There was a light at the entrance that gave good visibility throughout.

More exciting was the area underneath the house. There were about thirty inches between the ground and the floor. We had a small panel that matched the outside walls of the house that we could push aside to gain entry. There we stored Irish potatoes and onions that had been harvested from the garden, so that they would not rot or develop holes in their skin. It was cool and damp underneath the house with no direct sunlight, so the vegetables kept longer. This is where I kept my pole-vaulting pole that my dad made me. You could see the large black sewer pipes that went to the bathroom and the plumbing that served the kitchen. There were small holes in the walls that were covered with screen wire that let some light in and served as ventilation as well. It was a strange land beneath the house. There were concrete piers that held the house up. There was an odd musty smell under the house that never went away. It was kind of scary. I would crawl inside for a short distance. It was truly a special place for a kid to study. I didn't like to go too far because I was afraid I might encounter a snake.

31. GRASS MOWING AND FLOWERS:

The grass we had in the yard was mostly Bermuda grass that died in the summer when the weather turned hot, so we didn't have to mow all season, and we certainly never watered it to green up just to mow again. St Augustine grass had not arrived yet. Sometimes we got some late season rains and the grass greened up again in the fall. Our flowers were in the flower beds but many neighbors had flowers planted throughout their entire yard, so they did have to mow. Some yards had both, large flower beds and small areas of grass that had to be mowed. We always had plenty of cut flowers from the house for the cemetery on special occasions such a Mother's Day and Father's Day.

Mr. Charlie Berry, who lived in the house just north of us, had his entire yard either in a vegetable garden or a flower bed. He not only had annual plants, he also had perennials like iris and cannas that returned every year. He had many other varieties including morning glories that ran on the fences and poles. There was a red bud tree that grew near Franklin Street that was the first to bloom in the spring. There were a few people who had roses scattered in between the other plants or in a bed all to themselves. Some were climbers or made very large bushes and bloomed constantly all summer long. Mr. Charlie would hoe flowers and pull the weeds out and cultivate them but did not have to mow. My mother told me that our yard used to be the same way, that her father had grown flowers instead of a lawn. I got the full benefit of this because my Tate grandparents had a flower garden instead of a lawn.

The grass was mowed by a push mower. The blades had to be kept sharpened by a hand file. We had a large yard, and this was quite an effort every week to get the grass mowed. I can remember my father mowing the grass late in the afternoon and shortly after dark when it was cooler. By the time that I was old enough to mow, we had the gasoline power mowers that pulled themselves and made the job not only a lot faster but a lot easier. In time this was one of the responsibilities that I inherited as a member of our family. I actually enjoyed mowing the yard.

32. POETRY AND PROSE.

When my dad was going to school, he had to learn to recite poetry and prose by memory. And I used to think learning the Gettysburg Address was hard. His sister Dorothy Barnett told how my father used to stand before a mirror upstairs in the old homestead, reciting for hours things he was required to learn in school. One of my fondest memories of my dad was waking up on a spring morning and hearing him quote from Chaucer or in the fall reciting other rhymes.

Between the years 1387 and 1400, Geoffrey Chaucer, the Controller of Customs and a Justice of the Peace in England, wrote twenty-four stories known as the *Canterbury Tales*. They were written in Middle English. It was a part of a story telling contest by a group of pilgrims as they travelled together from Tabard Inn in London to Canterbury to visit the shrine of St. Thomas Becket. The host of the inn suggests that each member of the group tell a tale on the way to Canterbury in order to make the time pass more quickly. The tales would be judged and the winner would get a free dinner. My father's favorite was from the prologue. "Whan that Aprille with his shorers soote, that droughte of marche hath perced to the roote, and bached every veyne in swich licour, of which verba engendered is the flour." One of his other favorite tales was the Ploughman. He is a God-fearing man whose faith guides his life. It is why he leads a simple life though he has to work hard to do the direst of jobs. "Crystys modyr dere, that bare both God and man." I remember a few other phrases: "Gladly wolde he learne, and gladly teche" or "Love will not be constained by mastery." You could hear this broken English, verse after verse, coming from the back bedroom. It was my father's voice.

On cool mornings in the fall, my dad liked to quote from John Whitcomb Riley's poem "When the Frost is on the Pumpkin."

"When the frost is on the pumpkin and the fodders in the shock, and you hear the knock and gobble of the strutting turkey cock, and the cackle of the guinea and the clucking of the hen, and the roosters hallelujah as he tiptoes down the fence, and you leave the house bareheaded to go out and feed the stock, when the frost is on the pumpkin and the fodder in the shock."

These were all about farming or farmer's stories, which was my father and his family's occupation when he was growing up. He was not only memorizing verses of literature, but he was learning about the life and hardships of farm life. I heard them so often that I learned to quote them myself.

33. TAR TRUCKS AND FOGGING MACHINES:

Most streets were paved in the downtown area. The Tarrant County Commissioner for Pct. 3 helped the city maintain the streets. To repair the streets, they covered them with hot tar that was sprayed on from a large tanker, tar truck. After the thin cover of tar was sprayed on the road, it was topped with pea gravel. The pea gravel was pressed into the tar by the cars and helped form a solid surface for the streets. The County would come back in future years and fill any cracks that had occurred with tar that kept them sealed but it gave them a very definite patched look. In the summertime when the temperature got above 100 degrees, the tar on the streets would melt and when you walked on it barefoot, then tar would stick to the bottom of your feet. You did not want to walk on the pavement wearing good shoes or the tar would ruin them. You had to walk on the grassy shoulder. After the temperature cooled off by the time school started, back then the streets were stable again and remained that way for the rest of the year. Each time a new coat of tar and gravel was added it just added to the street base and made it stronger. Our streets didn't seem to have to be torn up and rebuilt, just overlaid. The highways were built differently with a six-inch gravel base and two and a half inches of hot mix laid over it and pressed by a big rolling machine.

If you walked the edge of the roadways or in the bar ditches, to avoid the wet tar, you encountered another problem and that was the goatheads. They are an invader of the plant family that grows on dry and gravelly soil, close to the ground. They have a deep tap root, with small yellow flowers and stickers that look like goatheads. They are very rough on animals and barefoot boys and girls. They grew throughout our neighborhood.

The other phenomenon of the summer was the fogging machine also provided by the County. It would come around several times in the summer for mosquito control. It usually arrived in the cool afternoon around sunset. It was an attractive nuisance. Like the bell on the ice cream truck, kids came running. You could see it coming because it put out a large cloud of white fog or what appeared to be smoke. They were using DDT which would later become a controlled substance because of its cancer-causing agents. We were ignorant back then so we would run and follow the truck and disappear in the cloud of smoke, laughing and being amused by every minute. All of the neighborhood kids came out and did the same thing. Oh, what fun this was. Later, mosquitos were controlled by fogging airplanes and sprayers in the back of trucks with a different, safer chemical used. It is done late at night when kids and parents are in the house or in bed. No one knows of anyone catching cancer from these old fogging machines but it is clear that chemicals are dangerous and that it was a foolish childhood game to play in the fog. DDT was sold over the counter and used in home pump sprayers that were used in every home to control flies. We live and learn.

34. HORSE APPLES

As kids we did not have a lot of store bought toys so we had to improvise and make our own elaborate toys. We depended on the natural resources of the area, particular by the back yard and neighborhood. We had Osage orange trees to the east and south. They made these large, green, uneatable apples in the fall that rolled all over the neighborhood in the wind.

These trees came from Solon Dunn's nursery when the trees where planted on the Grapevine Prairie to make hedges to hold cattle. When the seedlings were planted six inches apart in a row, after three years they would make a hedge that was horse high, pig thick, and bull strong. We could use these green apples that were about the size of soft balls to play catch with a friend or to chunk at each other in games of war, or you could roll them like bowling balls or push them with sticks like hockey pucks. They were a lot of fun. The problem was that they got rotten spots on them and if they got a hole in the skin then they leaked a white, milky substance that got all over your hands and clothes, which in turn got you in a jamb with your mother who had to wash it out on a rub board. With a large back yard and garden and all of the big trees to harbor game, my home was a hunting paradise for a kid.

35. DOODLE BUGS, MUD PIES, AND OLD WELLS.

My dad had a load of play sand dumped in our back yard to play with. Doodle bugs came with the sand and it was a lot of fun to take a small stick and try to lure them out. The doodle bugs made funnels in the sand and would go to the bottom of the funnel, covering their whole body with sand. The bug would then shake the sand off of his mouth, and wait for an ant to fall into the hole so he could eat it. We would say a rhyme, a chant at a doodle bug hole to try and get him to come up and show himself. Children would say, "Doodle bug, Doodle bug come out of your hole, your house is on fire and your children will die." Or "Doodle bug, Doodle bug, come to supper and I will give you some bread and butter." The doodle bug was a small, harmless creature. We also used the sand to mix with water and make mud pies. We made molds and made different objects out of the sand. I played with my sister "cooking" all kinds of fancy dinners. The sand pile was near old wells we had in the back yard before we had city water. It was the water supply for the property. The wells had been flattened at the ground and filled in, but they would settle from time to time and create a giant sink hole that we would have to be careful not to fall in before my dad filled it. The two wells were only a few feet apart and the cave ins only happened every few years.

36. CASE KNIVES

In the hardware store we sold a lot of pocketknives. We had them in a displace case and if a customer saw one they liked, then we looked at the number on the display and opened the back case and found that number and took a knife out of the box and let them look at it. One summer when I was about eight, my dad set me up with the case knives in a red wagon in front of the store. I set there and sold knives to customers all day Saturday. It was amazing how many people would stop and look at the knives even though they might not be in the market for one just because they were being displayed so conveniently by a little boy who was offering them for sale. I sold a lot of knives that day. We also sold Camillus Cutler knives that were in a separate display case. They were mainly smaller knives.

I liked to look at the knives. I would take them out of the box, unwrapping the brown tissue paper in which they were wrapped, and examine them to see if one looked better than the other ones. Many of the knives did vary from unit to unit. I always had the best looking knife I could find. The Case knife is still recognized for its quality around the world today. You can always tell a Case knife because it has the word "Case" inscribed on a small metal insert on each knife. The company also made a very large pocketknife with one or two blades that had a bone handle. They later became collector knives.

37. POLE VALUTING AND TELEPHONE WIRES

My father had been a good athlete in school, playing football, basketball, and doing the hurdles and high jump in track and field. When I was about ten years old, he made me a vaulting pole our of a large cane pole. It was ten feet long and about two inches around. I put black electric tape on the top end so my hands would not slip. I made a couple of post with nails on them to hold the cross bar which was also a smaller cane fishing pole. I didn't have a pit of sand to fall into so I had to land on the hard ground. This didn't stop me. It was a lot of fun and a real challenge to be able to vault higher and higher. I was lucky I did not break an arm or something. I practiced in the east front side yard and kept my equipment under the house. You would hope that by starting this young I would be very good by the time I got to high school. That was at least my dad's hope.

The side yard is where the telephone line came in from the street to the house. It was just the right height to throw balls over. One Christmas I got a kicking tee as a present and I practiced kicking the football over the telephone line. This was a lot of fun and easy to do, so I practiced a lot. I thought that I would probably be a kicker one day. I dreamed of becoming another Lou Groza from Ohio, who played professional football for the Cleveland Browns of the All-American Football Conference and later the National Football League. He played tackle but was also their place kicker for field goals and extra points. He was the best there was at the time. I enjoyed watching him on T. V. on Sunday afternoons. I guess this was Dad's hope too.

38. THE BACKYARD TREE

There used to be a lot of very large trees in the original part of town. Some had been planted by settlers and others had just grown there. There were all kinds, cedar, bor d' arc, and hackberry. The big tree in our yard was a giant hackberry that spread out over a large part of the back yard and house. It was magnificent, too big to climb. My parents always worried during ice storms that the limbs would break and damage the house. It was like a huge air conditioner and helped cool the house and yard to play in. It is where the swing was hung and where the clothesline connected to the fence post on the other end.

    I played many an hour under the shade of this old tree and fell in love with it. Here I made mud pies and dug for doodle bugs. Here was also the sight of many shower baths in summer from the old round sprinkle that was connected to the end of the garden hose. I shot at birds, primarily sparrows sitting on the limbs of the tree. It was under this tree that we sat in the summertime and cranked the old ice cream freeze and made homemade vanilla ice cream or cut a cold watermelon on a Sunday afternoon. It was under the tree that my mother's wash pot sat for boiling clothes which were then rubbed on a board, as well as where the chickens were killed and plucked and the black eyed peas were shelled. It is where my dog Jerry and my dad's birddog, Rex, would lie during the dog days of summer. Just outside of the canopy of the tree was our garden on the north and the lot where the cow, pig and chicken house was maintained.

    I can remember on winter nights lying in my bed in the back room and watching the dormant tree limbs blowing in the wind, the shadows it cast, and the moon that came up over the trees. I remember watching for the arrival of Santa Claus on Christmas Eve until I feel asleep. I could just imagine him arriving in his sleigh coming over the top of those wonderful trees.

39. BARN OWLS AND FIREFLIES

It seemed that there were more wildlife and insects around when the area was more rural, at least in the summertime, than when the city developed. Summer was a special time of the year because we spent more time outdoors and I enjoyed nature.

We had a lot more trees in town at that time. Even in our yard we had five large hackberry trees along College Street. I remember the Barn owls, which were very small owls that came out in the summer. I don't know where they nested, but at night they liked to sit in the hackberry trees and make their owl sounds.

They were not very wild and didn't seem to fly much. We usually saw several on a given night. My dad climbed up one of the trees one night and caught one to give me a closer look. The bird looked like a miniature hoot owl. They were about the size of a quail, but had big yellow eyes. My sister and I looked each owl over good before Dad placed it back in the tree. The barn owl didn't seem to have any natural enemies. But, over a course of time, the barn owls disappeared, not all at once, but fewer each year over a course of time. It was a fun spot to see the owls. It was part of what my sister and I did to entertain ourselves. It was a part of my childhood.

We sat out in the yard almost every night and slept out at times because it was cooler.

There were few lights at night, and it was very dark. During the hot months, a bounty of fireflies would come out just after dark. My sister and I liked to chase them. They were fast, dipping and diving, up and through the trees. At times there were too high and out of reach. I always wanted a butterfly net to give me an advantage, but when I finally owned one, I used it only for daytime hunting of butterflies.

40. ORION AND THE STARS

Because of the summer heat and lack of air condition, we often slept outside in the summertime. My dad had a small bed in the side or back yard, and sometimes I did too. We preferred the side yard so we could watch the foot and vehicular traffic on College Street, which was almost nonexistent back then.

After supper and about twilight, we would go outside. It was on these evenings that Dad taught me a lot. It was a good time for father and son. We would watch as the stars became more visible, trying to locate and identifying constellations before all of the stars were bright enough to see. Dad's favorite constellation was Orion, the hunter. I am not sure why it meant so much to him, but it must have dated back to his own childhood when he was growing up on the farm. It was there he became a pal and a friend of the "hunter."

Orion was very visible from our advantage point in the yard, clearly above the trees and almost overhead in the evening sky. The Big Dipper was also very visible, but the North Star was below the star line or very faint in our area in the summer. What we called the Evening Star, which I think was the planet Venus, was the first star we saw at night. There were only a few streetlights to interfere with the dark sky so the heavens were full of stars. On several occasions we would get the *World Book Encyclopedia* out to do research to try then to locate the various constellations and to visualize the imagines they represented.

Even in the humid days of July and August, it would get cool enough before morning to pull up a sheet or light blanket. Dawn would wake us, and we would return to our bed in the house for a few more winks of sleep before our day would begin

41. SWINGS AND SMOKESTACKS

The large hackberry tree in our backyard that offered a lot of opportunities growing up. Jerry, my dog, and I played under this precious tree. My swing was made from cow chain with a board for a seat. My sister and I took turns sharing the old swing in the backyard. I spent many an hour entertaining myself and seeing how high I could make the old swing go. I never did fall out of it or get above the limbs on the tree. Just in case of an accident, Dad hauled in a load of play sand. The sand also attracted doodle bugs, daring them to show their faces, a nice past time while resting from the swinging.

Just outside the radius of the swing was an old incinerator where we burned our trash. It had a fire box and then a chimney about five feet tall all made from brick. It also had a wash pot in the center where clothes were washed in hot water. I liked to climb on the chimney and get on top when the fire was not burning. I was always a climber, and I would climb anything if I could get my hands and feet on it.

One day I was climbing on the incinerator chimney watching my dad plant the garden and I pulled the chimney down on top of me. Lucky for me, it broke into pieces as it fell. Yes, it is a miracle that it was not the end of me. I was covered with bricks and bruises but more scared than hurt. No one had recognized that the chimney had deteriorated by time and weather. It was the scariest thing to happen in my small life. I realized how serious it could have been. It scared the daylights out of my mother as well. To say the least, the chimney was never rebuilt.

42. JONES STREET AND THE WEST END

Dad did most of the buying for the Tate Cash Stores, and though salesman came and went each week, and daily deliveries, Dad still always had to go to Dallas or Fort Worth to pick up special orders and to buy merchandise for weekend specials.

Dad always owned a green Chevrolet pickup truck. Sometimes it had sideboards on it for hauling a pig or cow, and other times it didn't. Before I started to school, I was traveling with my father on these weekly trips to buy merchandise. I was his companion but sometimes a nuisance. I asked a lot of questions. I learned a lot about life from my dad in the years I had him.

We would head for Ft. Worth, up highway 121 through Colleyville, Richland Hills, and Haltom City, then up Birdville Hill to Belknap Street, which took us downtown. We turned left off Belknap onto Jones Street. Our first stop would usually be Nash Hardware. We would back the truck up to the high concrete dock and climb the stairs to the first floor. The inside was dim with a lot of boxes stacked around that had an ink and packaging smell. We would go upstairs in the freight elevator to the sales office to sign the delivery receipt for our purchases.

Dad usually called the order in before we left, so it would be waiting for us when we arrived. There was an open elevator closed in by heavy wire on which the boxes of merchandise were brought down from upstairs. The boxes all had 'Nash Hardware' stamped on them by stencil. Our packages were labeled Tate Hardware with a felt pen. I would always look around for them among the array of boxes.

The Farmers Market was just south, down Jones Street where all the produce companies like Ben E. Keith Company, were located. Dad went shopping here to pick up seasonal items and to give a variety to the produce market in the grocery store.

Sometimes we would go to South Main to the Curtis Mathis distributor for fans, air conditioners, and parts. This would take us by Massey's, a restaurant which specialized in chicken fried steak, French fries, and homemade hot rolls. Dad liked to time his trip in the summertime for us to have lunch there. We always sat at the bar because the restaurant was always crowded. Occasionally, we would stop at a barbecue place on Belknap called Sammy's and eat a chopped barbecue sandwich. My dad seldom drank beer, but sometimes he would drink a long neck with a barbecue sandwich there.

On other days we would take a similar trip to Dallas along highway 114 past the Mustang Drive Inn, Moore's Wrecking Yard, past the WFAA Radio Station, and Dearing's Crossing at Belt Line Road, on to the traffic circle where we hit Harry Hines Blvd. Sometimes we stopped at Briggs Weaver on the way downtown, where we would purchase lawn mowers, small engines, and other parts. Then we would head for the west end of downtown Dallas where Huey and Phillips, Higginbotham Pearlstone, and Cullen and Boren were located. Cullen and Boren Company was a wholesaler of sporting and hunting equipment. The others were general merchandisers of hardwood goods.

When I started to school, I missed these trips except in the summer when school was out and on holidays. Of course, this was long before air conditioners were in the vehicles and it was very hot in the cities in the summertime. The only relief was a rolled down window and good conversation.

William D. Tate

43. I LOVED FLOWERS

As I have said before, people still planted flowers in their yards in lieu of grass because the push lawn mower was quite a physical challenge unless the grass was very short. To keep the grass short meant you had to mow twice a week. My Granddad Tate like others, had flowers all around his house. I loved flowers. I liked the various colors and the different shapes. I liked the experience of planting seed ad watching them sprout, grow and bloom. I enjoyed planting the gladiolus bulbs with my Granddad. The flowers attracted a lot of insects which meant there were a lot of Purple Martins around to feed on the insects. He also had several bee hives so there was a lot of nectar for the bees to harvest.

The flowers had to be tended to regularly to keep the weeds out, but since they had been cultivated for years, the weeds were not strong invaders. There were a lot of annual plants like snapdragons that grew about thirty inches tall and have fern like leaves with tall pink, purple, and white flowers. They bloomed all summer long. The poppy was another plant that returned each year and added a beautiful red to the flower garden. The poppy made a hard, green pod after it bloomed that was full of seed needed to replenish itself for the next year's crop. I never knew that the seeds were used for other things.

The periwinkle was one of my favorites. I remember they took a lot of sun and water. They were pink and white with dark green leaves. They would wilt down in the hot sun during the day and revive during the nighttime hours. They had to be watered every day. I thought the periwinkles were perennials because they were in the same place each year, but I learned later that they had to be replanted each year from seed.

I looked forward to seeing the pink blooms of the flowering quince that is the first bush to announce the coming of spring and the yellow blooms of the forsythia that soon follows. I also liked the rose bushes that bloomed all summer long, especially the red climbers that had a lot of blooms. They were usually planted up close to the house, and the blooms were often cut for house flowers. The snapdragon grew almost wild and was easy to maintain. They seemed to reseed themselves everywhere, and came in purple, pink and white.

The most common flowers were those of the crepe myrtle that came in white, red and pink.

When all of the various plants were in full bloom, their different colors made a beautiful garden for all to enjoy. People cut them daily so they always had fresh flowers in their houses. The flower garden yard was a frontier practice that died out during my childhood days.

44. CUB SCOUTS AND WEEBALO'S

My mother was our Cub Scout leader together with Louise Davis. She took me to Leonard Brother's in Fort Worth to buy me my uniform. There were about eight in my den. The Weebalo's Badge was the first I earned with the help of my mother. We met in our house in the dining room around the large round oak table. We had a handbook that we studied how to be a good citizen. We learned the scout salute. We learned to tie knots and how to camp. We had one overnight campout in Daivd Woolweaver's back lot. It was a great experience to cook out, and sit around a fire and tell stories and sleeping beneath the stars. We worked with silver and wood burning sets. We poured Plaster Paris into rubber molds to make our wolf, bear and lion as we advanced through the cub scouts. We also received various badges at a ceremony each year. I was always embarrassed when my name was called out and I did not like to participate in any activity in which I had to speak on in which attention was drawn to me. I was far from an exhibitionist. I showed no signs of showmanship. I was in fact terrified. Just the same it was a wonderful time of my life. My mother kept my awards in her cedar chest, and my handy work was hung on the walls of my bedroom. She stored away for safekeeping the display of knots, the silver work, and my wolf, bear, and lion patches so I would have memories from that time in my life.

Being a Cub Scout affected me a great deal. It impressed upon me to be kind and helpful to senior citizens, to be obedient to my parents and obey the law. I made a display of knots on a wooden board and wood burned a ship into a piece of wood to make a picture to hang on the wall. I have a paddle boat and a sailboat that I made which I used in the bathtub when I took a bath. One of our most iconic photographs was taken during my barefoot days wearing my Cub Scout uniform and standing next to my cousin Aubrey Eugene Wiley, wearing his army uniform during the Korean War.

45. CHRISTMAS TREES AND CANDY

One of the earliest jobs I had at the Tate Cash Stores was unbundling the Christmas Trees that arrived each year just after Thanksgiving. They would be wrapped together in bundles of six. Secured tightly with binder twine, they were sorted in accordance with height.

They were all white spruce and came in sizes from three to ten foot heights. Each height had a different color tag on the bottom branch so knowing the color code let you tell the height without measuring the tree. For example, the tags would be red, blue, green, yellow, white or purple.

I cut the binding and separated the trees in each bundle. They were bound as tight as possible to take up less room in shipping, so they lost their shape during transportation. I would take each individual tree and pull the branches downward so they would straighten themselves in the sunlight. They soon regained their shape. We built stands of wood to mount the trees on. They sold for $0.25, $0.50, $0.75, $1.00, and $1.25.

Soon other type trees became available, including Scotch pine and blue spruce. These trees had larger trunks and were harder to mount. My dad would pick up scrap lumber from A.J. Harper and J.B. Daniels building sites, and we would cut the boards, crossed them, and nailed them together. Then we would take a two-inch barrel arguer and bore a hole down the middle. We would have to trim the bottom of the trunk of the tree with a pocket-knife to fit the hole in the stand. After the tree was mounted, we would drive a large nail in the center to hold in on. The trees always had a wonderful forest aroma that I enjoyed each fall.

Christmas was always big on Main Street. It provided an opportunity for the merchants to sell a lot of different products that were not handled all year long. The store windows were decorated with Christmas wishes. School organizations would sponsor a Cookie Crawl on a Saturday during the holidays. Churches sent carolers out at night to sing to the residents. People began to put their Christmas trees in front of windows so people passing by could enjoy their trees too.

In addition to the smell of the Christmas trees, the seasonal candies were also very fragrant. Lemon drops, orange slices, nuts, and chocolates came in big cardboard boxes. The boxes than were opened, and the candy put in a glass covered walnut case in the grocery store. As the candy was sold, it was scooped into a brown paper sack and weighed. You could buy it by the pound or quarter pound. The candy provided one of the smells of Christmas that I will never forget.

The sounds and smells of Christmas were evident everywhere in the hopes that Old Saint Nicholas would soon be here.

46. SANTA CLAUS AND CHRISTMAS EVE

Christmas was an exciting time. With the seasonal sales in the stores, my father had extra money around Christmas time, so we always had a big Christmas. When my dad was a child, a new pair of socks or working boots, if the crops were good, was his only Christmas present. He wanted more for his family and the times after the war provided the opportunity.

Christmas Eve was also my father's birthday, so it was truly a time of celebration. There were other people on Main Street that shared the Christmas Eve birthday with my dad, including Wiley Willhoite and Mrs. Jim Bussey. They celebrated all day up and down the 400 block of Main Street with cake and cigars. Unless Christmas was on Sunday, when the stores were closed because of the Texas Blue Sky laws, the stores stayed open until 8 o'clock P.M. for the last- minute shoppers, so we did not open our presents until after Dad came home. We sold as lot of knives, Texas nutcrackers, hand warmers, television sets, linoleum rugs, rods and reels as last minute Christmas presents. Mother would light the stove in the living room where the tree was. It was one of the few times we used the front room during the wintertime. We would first have dinner, then Dad would open his birthday presents first and then we would open our Christmas presents and dream of Santa just a few hours away.

My stocking was hung on the right side of the mantel and Sandra's was on the left end. Santa was the one that brought most of our toys. The wrapped presents were mostly clothes. I could hardly wait until it was time to go to bed on Christmas Eve and then I had a hard time going to sleep. I usually got up about daylight and went in and got my gifts from Santa and brought them back into my mother's bedroom to play and enjoy them. Our tree was always in the living room, except for one year after we added on the den, Mother wanted to have a short tree on a table to show through the picture window. I always liked a bigger tree. The tree was in the corner by the window seat until Mother added a picture window in the living room, and then it sat in the center of the front wall.

Mother put our nativity scene on the mantle, but other than the tree, this was our decoration. Lights on the outside of the house had not become a custom. We used the same decorations each year. It was apart of our Christmas tradition. Mother always decorated the tree, usually when my sister and I were at school. It was a wonderful surprise to come home from school and find he tree decorated. She also was the one to take it down. If I was present, I liked to help her decorate the tree. First came the lights, the small antique shaped lights. Then we had bubble lights that when they heated up made bubbles inside the globe. Then we got even larger lights when they became available. When something new came out, we always sold it at the stores, which meant we had the same new products at home, too.

Our tree decorations were several deer, birds, and other animals, old fashion glass balls, and a few odds and ends, collections of many Christmases past. Some even might have been hand me downs from my mother's parents.

Mother made Sandra and me red felt stockings that hung on the mantel. The fireplace was not used, but it had a tan, fire proof cover. The cover went over the front. I think it was made out of asbestos to keep it from burning. Our front room was not kept warm in the wintertime except when we were using the room. We had a small gas heater that provided the heat.

I was always excited about Santa Claus, reading Christmas books, and coloring books for weeks before. Some of our gifts were homemade. The first years the presents were all wrapped in tissue paper without boxes. The paper came in blue, red, green, and white. We used the small ribbons of similar colors to secure the packaging. I could usually guess all my presents before Christmas. I would go into the living room when no one was watching and feel and shake my presents until I figured them out. Mostly, they were socks or shirts. I think it bothered my mother that I always seemed to know what she was giving me. She, of course, wanted it to be a surprise.

Santa always came. He left my presents in the big chair that sat by the fireplace. He didn't arrive until nearly morning; because I got up several times in the dark and found out he had not been there yet. Sometimes I would just lie awake in the big bed waiting for morning. I am sure I snoozed off for a while, but I was always excited.

Early in the morning, I would go into the living room in the dark. I remember it was always very cold. I could see my presents in the dark and that my stocking wasn't still hanging on the mantle. It was such a thrill. I would take a gift at a time into the middle bedroom that was warmer and start playing with it. My parents would still be trying to sleep because they were tired from the Christmas rush.

Santa brought me a lot of gifts over the years. I got a Lincoln Log set one year, and some Tiddlywinks. One of my favorites was a shooting gallery. It had a wire across the backstop on which you placed black plastic crows, on the wire. There was a slot on the crows to slip over the wire. I had a gun that shot a cork. You pumped the gun up and shot at the crows. If the cork hit a crow it would spin until it fell off. When I was eleven years old, Santa brought me a basketball game that had a red ping ball. It had a court with nets on each end. When you pulled on one of the wires on each side it would shoot the ball at the goal. There was a score board on each end to keep score. I also got an electric football game the next year. You plugged it in to the wall socket and the playing field vibrated. There were eleven players on offense and eleven on defense. There was a little white cotton football that the runner carried. You could also pass. When you player got the ball over the goal like it was a touchdown. We also got fireworks, sparklers and Roman candles in our stockings. I always liked the sparklers the best because I didn't need my parents to use them. The other fireworks were more dangerous and required parental supervision. There were always some apples and oranges that seemed to be bigger than the ones we sold in the store.

I don't remember too much about Santa visiting my sister. I know she got some dolls and dolls clothes and a doll sewing machine and things like that. I don't think my sister ever got as excited as I did about Santa Claus or her Christmas playthings. I was a bundle of energy and made up for her reluctance. I dreamed of Christmas all year long.

47. ICE IN THE WATER BUCKET.

The house that I grew up in was built by my maternal Grandfather Bennett. The same grandfather that had been a night watchman. He built a more modern house to replace the farmhouse that he lived in before. Yet when it was built, it had no bathroom or indoor plumbing and the cook stove was fueled by wood. By the time I arrived, we no longer used the outhouse, but instead had a bathroom with a commode and bathtub. There was plumbing in the kitchen for hot and cold water. The plumbing was under the house that stood up off the ground about thirty inches allowing the air to get very cold under the house in the winter. Any time that the temperature was to get below freezing, we had to go to the cut off in the front yard where water came in from the city meter and cut it off to the house and then drain the pipes to keep them from freezing. Mother would first draw water in the bathtub for flushing the commode and heating to wash dishes with, and she also filled a galvanized bucket in the kitchen to cook with. Mother always got up to cook Dad and the kids a good breakfast before we left to work or school. There was no fire in the kitchen except the kitchen stove. She got up many a morning in a cold house and went into the kitchen in her bathrobe and cooked a big breakfast when the water in the kitchen water bucket was frozen solid.

48. PATHFINDER and FLOWERSACK

Both of these words have ten letters all of which are different. Pathfinder was the code that we used in Tate Hardware and Tate Grocery to mark the cost of an item on the box or merchandise. All stores had similar inventory codes. Flowersack was the code used by my mother in her store, Louise's Variety. With this information, if we wanted to give a price break, we knew how much we could give. It was also important in the taking of inventory at the end of each year. We would count the number of items and list the cost. That times the total number would give us the cost of the inventory. For example, an item marked AFR in the hardware would mean that the item cost $2.50 each.

One of my jobs was restocking. I knew where every item went. When the truck came in with a delivery, then I would open up the merchandise, check it, mark it, and then put it out on the shelves. If the item had gone up, then I had to mark the sales price up on the same existing merchandise. In this way we controlled our inventory.

Heat, cold, or water did not remove the markings, though they could be smeared if you rubbed hard enough. This, of course, was before computers and other more efficient forms of inventory maintenance.

49. BIBLE SCHOOL AND WASH TUBS

Once every summer we had Vacation Bible School at the Methodist Church where my family worshipped. The bell on the tall wooden tower at the northwest corner of the church would ring every morning to remind parents to bring their children. The bell could be heard through out the town proper, but, of course, not in the outlying rural areas.

Bible School was a week long, and it took place in the very heat of summer. My mother was often a leader in the organization, production, and teaching of the school. We would study Bible lessons in the basement of the church or in the log cabin next door, called Leach Hall. The basement was not air conditioned. It had concrete outside walls and windows in each classroom just above the ground. That concrete helped keep the basement cool.

After class we would then go outside for recess and refreshments. My dad often provided refreshments from the store, including cookies and soft drinks. Dad would take a couple of number two washtubs and fill them with all kinds of soft drinks—Dr. Pepper, Coca Cola, Pepsi, 7-Up, Big Red, Orange Crush, and root beer, and then cover them with crushed ice from the ice plant. By the time recess arrived, they were as cold as could be. We played games like softball and pop the whip and jump rope. The students sought the shelter of the big oak trees for relief from the heat. We also had some refreshments on site before we went home.

Under the shade of the Vitex trees in front of the church is where the refreshments were unloaded and passed out as parents came to pick up their children. Vacation Bible School ended with a program on Sunday night to show our parents what we had done during the week. It was something we looked forward to each year.

50. BBs, REVOLVERS, AND A 410

Dad and Granddad Tate were hunters so I was always around their guns. I knew not to bother the guns even though they were always unloaded. I didn't have access to ammunition.

I often looked at and admired the guns. Dad kept his in the closet in the back of the hardware store, both his 20 gauge LC Smith shotgun and his 250-3000 Savage deer rifle. My grandfather had a 20 gauge Remington automatic shotgun that was often propped up against the back wall inside the screened-in porch at his house on Wall Street.

I knew I would be a hunter at an early age, so I needed to be learning about these sorts of things and paid a lot of attention to the talk and the equipment. My first gun was a wooden gun with a clothes pin on the back that shot large rubber bands made from old inner tubes. I don't think my dad made the gun. I think he bought it from a customer.

This was a neat gun, but I soon learned it was not as accurate as I would like. I shot it at rocks, tin cans, and toad frogs. I then graduated to cap pistols and holsters like the real cowboys such as Roy Rogers, Gene Autry, Hopalong Cassidy, and the Lone Ranger wore. I had several of these silver pistols before my time was gone. I even ordered a complete outfit from a coupon on a box of Cheerios. I got a double set of Lone Ranger pistols, holsters, cuffs, vest, and chaps.

The caps made a loud sound when the trigger was pulled, and fire sometimes came from the gun. It was pretty real. The caps came in small cardboard boxes with about eight rolls attached together, usually on red paper. You would separate a roll, then break your pistol open for loading. The cap roll fit over a metal bar. You threaded the cap up through the back of the gun finally coming to rest under the hammer. The caps self threaded as each one was fired, so you got off several shots in a hurry, like a Colt 45.

Then one year for Christmas, Santa Claus brought me a Red Raider BB gun. This was really a weapon. You loaded the BBs down a tube so you could get several shots. The BBs came in round tubs of 100s or 200s. These were popular guns like the 30-30. They would even kill a sparrow if you hit it right, though I never took a sparrow's life. Dad told me that all the birds had a purpose for being on earth. Dad began teaching me gun safety. I hunted the trees of the backyard. I had to be very careful because I knew my dad would take the gun away, if I did not obey the rules. I knew this was important because I had often heard the story about my dad getting shot in the lip with a BB when he was a child. I learned not to point the gun at something you didn't want to kill. You never pointed the gun towards a human being. You also didn't shoot over someone's house or at someone's dog or cat.

Then came the 410 shotgun to go hunting for dove. A single shot with a hammer. It made me nervous because when you cocked the hammer and didn't get a shot you had to lower it without the gun firing. I never will forget when I killed my first dove with this gun, even though I am sure until this day, that it was just luck. We were hunting in a sunflower patch just off of Belt Line Road when the bird came from my right and crossed in front of me. Once you have taken your first bird, it gives you a calm confidence which makes the next shot a lot easier.

51. OLD DOGS AND WATER BARRELS

My first recollection of a family pet was a small black, white, and brown dog, a male dog, whose most distinct markings came from his fox terrier bloodline. He name was Jerry. Jerry was a member of our family before I was born. Dad, of course, had his bird dog named Rex who was a liver and white English pointer. They were both good pets for young children. We had Jerry about eight years before he left us. He was more my sister's dog.

I went to a party at Mrs. Martin's house on Ball Street after Jerry died. They had a litter of puppies from small cross breeds. A white one caught my attention. I went home and after a long battle for persuasion, talked my parents into letting me have the puppy. We named her Patti. We only had her a few years. She got into some poison and died a terrible death one night in the back bedroom.

After Patti came a little Mexican chihuahua that was so small I could nearly put him in my pocket. We named him Mickey. He could jump up on the bed or anything else in the house. He slept with one of the family every night. My dad liked to take him to the farm that we had just acquired. One day at the farm, my dad ran into Mickey while trying to catch a chicken and broke one of his front legs. We tried to get his leg set but it would not heal. Finally, we had to have his leg amputated. Then we had a three-legged dog for a pet.

At this time wooden water barrels were still popular. Metal cans had hit the market, but we still sold several sizes of wooden water barrels that workmen used to ice down with cold water during the day. We had to keep these wooden barrels filled with water or the staves would shrink, and the barrel would fall apart. They were fine when they were new because they had a coating that sealed them for a while. They had a half lid on top and a value on the bottom to drain the water into a glass. I used to display these wooden water barrels on the sidewalk outside the hardware in the summertime. Dad had a large wooden barrel he had bought that we used during Vacation Bible School and large events. It sat under the big hackberry tree in the backyard. It was one of my jobs to keep water in it to keep it solid. You didn't have to fill the barrel up, but you needed about a foot of water in it so the water would traverse up the wood to the top of the barrel and keep the barrel rings tight. One summer I forgot to take care of the water in the barrel and it fell apart. You can't expect too much for, after all, I was just a kid.

52. COWBOYS AND INDIANS

During my barefoot days, a lot of the movies and later the T.V. shows were based on cowboy and Indian tales. As the result of that we liked to play the games between cowboys and Indians. We had our cap pistols and holster and our cowboy outfits; and we made our bows and arrows and took off our shirts and played the role of Indians. We had our stick ponies. We had our cowboy hats. We had our silver bullets. We had our sling shots and chinaberries. We had all of the real equipment that we needed. It was as realistic as it gets. We chased each other around the house and hid in the bushes, trying not to be found and trying not to get shot, imagining and playing out our fantasies. We would throw our ropes and pull cowboys off their horses, then lock them up for stealing ponies. We would come out of the barns and off the rooftops in surprise, scaring the tar out of everyone, with a few frightening yells, and have a jolly good time. We could do the war whop when we came running out in ambush of the white folks. We could play that our horse would rare up like the Lone Rangers. We could play like we were his side kick, Tonto. We could shoot our arrows and pop our cap pistols and play like we had been shot. These were the days before Little League baseball and football and before the fireman and the policemen became a child's idol, which was what children wanted to become when they grew up.

53. PIANO LESSONS AND RECITAL

We had my mother's piano that sat in the living room between the two front windows, on the front wall of the house. When we opened the front door to the left, it gave us a good breeze and a better light to see the keyboard. I used to go to the living room and bang on the keyboard, something we were not permitted to do because it caused the piano to be out of tune. I guess I was the villain, because I can remember my mother having the piano tuner come by every couple of years and tune it. I watched the tuner do his work, but I never quite figured it out on how he fixed it. He opened up the lid in front and exposed the moving parts that made the sound. He seemed like he knew what he was doing. Then one fall my mother got the idea that since I liked to "play like" I was playing the piano, that she would pay for me to have private lessons with Ms. Madeline Hemley where my sister had been taking lessons for several years. She lived at 513 Dooley Street in a white frame house, and she had a piano in the living room where we took our lessons. Ms. Hemley was also the music teacher at the Grapevine Public Schools and very dogmatic.

My mother could play the piano very well and played at Eastern Star and at the First Methodist Church. Her mother had been a piano player, and other family members had played in a local band in the band stand on Main Street. I guess my mother thought that I should be a part of the musical family. She even bought me a ukulele but I never learned to play it either. Somehow, I just never caught on to the idea about playing a musical instrument. It didn't seem to me to be a boy thing. It is what the girls did. I never practiced at home, and my mother let me get by with every excuse. Then at the end of the school year we had what was called a recital when we would show our parents what we had learned from the lessons for the year. This is when the birds came home to roost. My teacher picked out a couple of songs for me to play, and we practiced but I stumbled every time and did not have any confidence that I could do it. I had a hard time reading the notes. The recital was at night at Ms. Hemley's house. All of our parents were there. The participants waited for their turn in a holding room out of sight. As my time got closer and closer, I became more and more nervous and my hands began to sweat. I thought I was having a heart attack. This is the first time the fear of God had passed over me. I was scared to death. Finally, my turn came, and I walked proudly into the front room and sat down at the piano knowing full well how bad it was going to be. I did not disappoint anyone. My parents must have been humiliated. I banged and skipped notes throughout the presentation knowing that this was it. I determined that I was never putting myself in this position again. Not much was said on the way home that night. I told my mother later that I didn't want to take piano lessons anymore and I didn't. Of course, I regret it now because I cannot play the piano and show off.

54. THE CREPE MYRTLE TREE

One day it just happened. I realized that I could shimmy all the way up the old crepe myrtle tree on the east side of the house. I had been climbing it for years but not all the way to the roof. My fear was not getting onto the roof but getting back down. It took a lot of courage to make that last leap of faith. Once on top of the house, I could walk all around and inspect the lightning rods that were scattered about to ground the house. In the event of a lightning strike, the electricity would run into the ground rather than setting the house on fire. I was amazed at the sights I could see from the top of the house. I could see over my entire kingdom with little effort. I knew my mother did not want me on the roof so I had to be very careful. She was not as afraid that I might fall off the roof as much as she was concerned that I might do damage to the shingles by walking on them. I just wasn't that heavy. I would sit up there for a while, just enjoying the view and intrigued by the danger. Coming down for the first time was a little testy, but I learned to wrap my legs around the limbs and hold on for dear life. I used this old tree that had such beautiful rose-colored floors all summer, for many of my purposes. I could take a knife and outline any pattern I wanted and then lift the bark right off in one piece. For example, I could make a scabbard for my knife. I would take the bark off and then sew it up with plastic string that I got in Cub Scouts. Sometimes I just carved my initials BT in the bark or made hearts that said, "I love you." Then one day many years later in a dry year the old crepe myrtle tree died. I was so sad because it held so many memories. The dead branches were cut away. But the next year I looked out and to my surprise the old tree had sprouted from its roots. It took a few years, but the old tree came back for a second life. All I can do now is enjoy the pretty blooms.

55. RABBITS AND HOMEMADE CAGES

During the time that I did not have a dog, my dad got me a couple of rabbits from a friend. It was a new experience, another delectation. Dad had my Uncle Arthur Tate build me a rabbit cage which was very nice. It had a closed part in the back for the rabbits to get out of bad weather and then a screened cage in front made out of hardware cloth. The roof and the enclosed part were covered with sample of roofing shingles that they gave us at the lumberyard. The back had a door that rose up from the bottom and the front had a upright door where I could feed and water the rabbits. I was cutting up some lettuce for the rabbits with my pocket- knife and cut a deep cut in my left thumb. My parents were not home, and I was able to bandage the cut and stop the bleeding without my parents knowing. By the time they discovered my cut, it was too late to get stiches. I still have a disfiguring scar on my left thumb.

One day I noticed a lot of hair in the back of the cage and opening the back door I found that my rabbit had had four babies. Their eyes were closed, and they had no hair on their bodies and I did not know not to touch them, which I did, and then the mother abandoned them and they died. I felt so guilty. My dad assured me that it would not be long before the mother rabbit had another litter and he was right. This time I left them alone and got to enjoy watching the babies grow up. My Uncle Arthur also made some cages for my bantam chickens, that were similar, except they set on the ground where they could move around so the chickens could eat fresh grass. These cages also had a closed in area in the back with a roof that opened as a door, where I could collect the eggs.

56. SATURDAY DRAWINGS AND COUPONS

The local merchant association came up with the idea of drawings on Saturday afternoons for prizes as a hedge against people trading in other communities like Lewisville or Euless and against new and larger stores that were beginning to show up. So with each 25 cents purchased in a participating store, you got a numbered ticket off of a roll of tickets. The businesses gave prizes to draw for like a skillet or a knife or a piece of clothing. On Saturday afternoons there was a drawing under the water tower across from the movie theater. People would collect their tickets and drop them in a big turning wheel and a special person would be chosen to reach in and pick a ticket for each prize. The tickets had a number on each end, so they were torn in half and to win you had to have the companion piece of the ticket with the winning number printed on it. There were large crowds for the drawings, and they were a big success. It brought more people to town and people enjoyed being a winner even back then. During the week a representative would go by each store and collect the prizes that they wanted to give each week and the prizes would be on display during the drawing. After the drawing people gathered and visited and conversed about the news, or some would go to the movie theater and others just went home to try out their new prize.

57. THE WIZARD OF OZ

I must have gone to the movies a lot with my mother when I was very young because I can remember the newsreels about what was going on in WWII. I was three when it was over. It was interesting that I would remember the news and the cartoons but nothing about any of the movies that I went to see. That all changed one night when my parents took my sister and me to see a movie called *The Wizard of Oz*. There was a large crowd that night, so we had to sit in the balcony. The movie started out with a tornado which blew the farm away and took Dorothy to Oz. It was so scary I could hardly watch. Then there was the Lion, the Tin Man, the Scarecrow, and the Witch. It didn't get any better for me. They were all very scary. My parents seemed to like it with the rest of the crowd. I guess looking backward it was very entertaining. To me, it was real and frightening, especially for Dorothy and her dog. I kept getting under the seat or closing my eyes. I am sure I ruined it for my mother who was probably embarrassed by my behavior. I watched the show many times after that first experience and realized it was just make-believe, not real. After this realization, I could enjoy the show and appreciate that it was one of the classic movies of all time.

58. PORCH SWINGS AND SUMMER EVENINGS

As did most houses when I was a kid, our house had a front porch. On the front porch was a platform swing that my mother and sister and I sat in a lot in the summer and swung back and forth. It was an unusual swing because most of them swung from chains attached to the ceiling instead of on a platform that sat on the porch. I don't know where or when we got the swing, but it was a fixture and was always there until it finally wore out and fell apart. My dad worked late on Saturday evenings because the stores stayed open until 9 o'clock. That left mother with the job of entertaining two kids. The swing in summertime was a sure bet. We also just sat in the swing and watched people walk up and down the street. We engaged in a lot of conversation or jibber-jabber and visited among ourselves. It was a way of life.

Ernest and Bonnie Lowe who lived across the street also had a front porch, and they set out on the porch almost every evening when it was warm enough. I would go over and visit with them and talk. They had built the house in 1916 and moved to town from the farm. Both of them smoked, something I didn't really like but most people did back then. I remember Mr. Lowe used a cigarette holder but still had brown stains on his index finger from smoking. He was very tall and industrious. He once won the Tall Man Contest in the city in conjunction with the opening of Northwest Highway in Grapevine. His nickname was "Shorty." Shorty worked at Spinks Drug Store and was Mayor of Grapevine from 1924 to 1932. During his tenure he passed bonds to build a city water system and also a sewer system. He issued long term franchises for telephone, gas, and electricity. As Shorty grew older, he slowed down. He was not void of energy or limp-wristed, but he walked with the speed of a jellyfish. It didn't seem to bother him that I roamed the neighborhood, so he didn't alter my behavior. The Lowes did not have any chicken house or garden, so the front porch and the candy dish was their greatest draw.

Sometimes we had watermelon on these evenings or had a picnic outside. Other times Mother dressed up and took Sandra and me downtown. We walked Main Street and visited with the customers. On weekday evenings we mowed the yard or tended to the flower beds or listened to the radio. Sometimes on Sunday afternoon the Wileys (mother's sister) would come from Ft, Worth to visit with us. Talking was a big pass time back then.

59. POTTERY AND BIRD BATHS

An itinerant merchant sold Dad some concrete flowerpots, benches, and bird baths. We put them around the picket fence in the backyard. People driving by would stop, and I would sell them pottery, even though I was hardly big enough to lift some of the items.

This is the way that I got started in the backyard business. I became an entrepreneur. The bird baths went first. There were so heavy my mother didn't want to keep one, because she was afraid I would turn it over on me and hurt myself. She kept a concrete pot and bench instead. When this inventory was nearly gone, Dad bought a large shipment of a different kind of pottery, from Marshall Pottery Company in Marshall, Texas. They delivered it in a big truck right to the back yard.

I put a lot of the pottery items on the concrete benches. We priced the items with a felt pen. There were several kinds and sizes of pitchers, churns, mixing bowls, rabbit feeders, and waterers. The feeders were turned in at the top to hold the feed in better. The waterers were straight. We had bird baths, churns, water jugs with faucets, bowls of all sizes, and mugs. I sold these for many years.

The pottery got dirty setting out. We tried to keep them turned over so they wouldn't fill with rainwater, but there was always a customer who left the top up and I would have to empty them after every rain. The vitex trees also lost leaves that would go into the pottery if they were not turned upside down. It was an occupational hazard. Customers would not buy under these types of circumstances today. They would want the merchandise clean. It was a constant business to manage. We had no sign or advertisement. Zoning laws would now preclude this type of family business in a residential area.

I kept change in a cigar box, and I never took a bad check. I kept my own inventory and let Dad know when I needed a new shipment.

60. VITEX AND BADMINTON

We had several vitex trees in the back yard. One by the garbage cans at the driveway. Another one had a limb that ran parallel to the ground that I used to climb out on and lie there like a lion waiting for his prey. This is the tree on the cover of the book.

We had two other groups of vitex trees on either side of this tree, all behind the picket fence that separated the front yard from the back yard. In the east side yard there was another vitex tree. It was to this tree that we tied our badminton net to on one side and to the pomegranate tree on the house side. It was perfect for this purpose. I also could climb in this vitex tree because it had many branches at the ground level.

I liked to play badminton, a game given to me about my ninth Christmas. We didn't leave the net up but put it up for special occasions like birthday parties. It was up for my tenth birthday, but I had the measles and had to cancel the party.

My dad and sister also liked to play badminton. It was a good game. Badminton is a racquet sport played with rackets to hit a shuttlecock or bird across a net. The racket is like a tennis racket but lighter. It is played as singles or doubles. You try to hit the bird high in the air and over the net. Points are scored when the bird lands in bounds on the other side of the net. The game itself was kind of a cross between volleyball and tennis. Some of my cousins would also play with me. It was one of the few outside games that we had.

Croquet was the other one. Croquet is a sport using wooden balls with different colored strips on each one, driven by a mallet through a hoop or "wicket" embedded in the ground on a grass court. There was a stake at each end of the court. After you completed the course, you had to knock the ball through a double hoop and hit the stake to win the game. It was invented in England where the rich played against the poor. In our case it was the old against the young. You got a free shot after you knocked the ball through the hoop. My dad liked to play croquet. It was one of the few games he played with us. We set it up on the east front yard. The equipment sat on the front porch for years. We finally lost interest as we grew older, and somewhere along the way the equipment disappeared.

61. WATER FANS AND SHEETS

The house I grew up in on West College had high ceilings and a lot of windows to allow for air circulation in the summer months. It was a good thing that my parents understood the importance of this design, or we would have all perished in the summer heat in our childhood.

For hundreds of years the opening of windows, creating a cross ventilation, in the spring and summer, was the only chance to get relief from the unbearable heat. But during my youthful years, a grand invention came along that would change the world in just a few years. It was called the evaporated cooler. It was a fan that came out after WWII and was packaged in nicely finished wooden cases. It was larger than the small oscillating electric fans that we had before or the ceiling fans in stores. What was special was that you could hook water up to them. You accomplished this by attaching a metal rack to the outside of the window where the window screen used to hang. Inside the metal rack was an excelsior pad made from very small round stripes of wood that looked like coils of string. Then 1/4-inch copper tubing hooked a water drip line up to the metal frame. The water then shifted or dripped down through the pad and collected in a pan at the bottom that was drained off by a water hose. The fan then sucked air from outside through the wet pad and into the room in the house, a process which had the result of cooling down the house. It worked. It was a dream. It was clever. Of course, as the pad began to mildew and age, it smelled a little bit, but who cared anymore if it made you cooler. The pads were replaceable and came in various sizes.

We got in the habit of staying up late at night because the air usually got cooler and the sleeping would be better. We then made up for staying up late by sleeping later in the morning, when our home spun apparatus was in full use. We took the top sheet on the bed and tied the corners to the four posters of the bed forming a tent that would trap the cooler air and make it hang around longer. Weren't we geniuses? Like the ancient mariners we attached our sails and drifted into a better life. I have always liked to stay up late and sleep in of the morning as the result of this evolution.

62. BICYCLE PATHS AND SIDEWALKS

Dad bought me a Lone Ranger bicycle when I was big enough to ride it, perhaps around the age of twelve years or so. I had not learned to ride a bicycle on a smaller one with training wheels. The bicycle was maroon and cream colored with white sidewall tires. It had a wire basket in front to carry things in, but I didn't use the basket that much. We kept my sister's bike and mine on the front porch. We did not lock them or chain them to the floor because we had very little crime around the neighborhood.

A sidewalk led from our front porch to the sidewalk that ran parallel to College Street on one side with the five large hackberry trees on the other. There were no adjoining sidewalks, so it was a path that led to nowhere. I rode my bike up and down the sidewalk until I nearly wore the sidewalk out. My sister had a blue girl's bicycle and she sometimes rode with me. We made some trails through the front yard that we also rode on, creating bumps and moguls throughout the path to make it more challenging. There were sidewalks along College Street, but not on Church or the other streets near our house. We were not allowed to ride in the street because it was considered too dangerous. Therefore, we did not get to ride our bicycles to school, to church, to downtown, or to our friends' houses. We walked instead. My mother did not get her driver's licenses until after I started to school, and Dad was always working and did not have the time to drive us where we were going.

I took a few spills learning to ride this big bicycle, but the ones that hurt the most came later, when I would wreck because I was going too fast or got careless and was not watching where I was going.

I got a maroon license plate for my bicycle and attached it to the back fender. I really thought I had arrived and could take to the streets once I was licensed. I had ordered it from an advertisement on a box of cereal.

63. THE SHEDS

The thing that distinguished Grapevine's historic district when I was growing up was the outbuildings. The one-car garages, small barns, tool sheds, privies, and hen houses sitting on large lots.

We had a one-car garage that sat near the street, that I have already talked about, an outhouse, barn and chicken house. They were all made of wood with the small green shingle roof just like our house except the barn which had a tin roof and sides. The outhouse set beside the chicken house. The outhouse was used to store building supplies, tools, nails and paint.

The Berrys had a car but did not drive it very much. They used their barn as a tool shed to store hoes, rakes and such stuff, and canned goods. All of their outbuildings were unpainted wood. They used the shed next to the garage and henhouse to store vegetables that they had canned. They were kept in cardboard boxes and labels, peas, carrots, beans, etc. There was a large barn on the Oscar Thomas place to the east. It was used for a garage and the storage of old magazines, newspapers, and the like. It was open and had a treasure trove of opportunities. Our barn sat on the back of the property. The tool sheds were usually locked and off premises for most of my life.

Just down Church Street was as large wood frame barn setting on a lot without a house. It was used to store hay in the loft. It was off limits for me and I only admired it from the street and often wondered what treasures might await inside.

64. MRS. PARR AND ABC'S

In my day the teachers did not want the parents to start trying to teach their kids. They were afraid, I guess, that they would teach them the wrong way or would allow bad habits to be adopted, that the teacher would have to unteach. At any rate, Mrs. Willie D. Parr was my first grade teacher. She appeared to be about my mother's age and had dark hair that was beginning to show a few gray strains, and a gruff voice that would scare a cat off the roof.

    I never will forget my first day in school. I was not that excited, because I had already established my free life style roaming the neighborhood and developing my interest. I could see very quickly that public schooling was going to interfere with, if not completely destroy, what I had spent my first six years accomplishing. School meant the loss of my freedom and my independence. My self-confidence went out the window too. I became timid and was embarrassed to speak when the teach asked me a question during class. Like a calf that had been roped, tied and branded, there was no escape. My mother was glad to see me start to school. She saw me as a rover, like a free ranging chicken, and a little strong headed. She thought school would be good for me. The teacher assigned me a seat at one of the long tables where about eight students would spend the year. These were working desks, designed for coloring and such as that. Above the blackboards there was, wrapped around the room, the ABC's in both small and capital letters. I had never heard of such a thing and was somewhat taken back. After all I had learned to talk and was able to communicate quite nicely without reference to the alphabet. I could not imagine why I would need to possess such knowledge. I thought comic books and the Golden Books were just to look at the pictures. I had never considered such a thing as possessing the skill of reading. It was the beginning of the rest of my life.

    Mrs. Parr made it clear from the start, there would be no talking with the other students, getting out of your seat without permission, or leaving the room to go to the restroom except as a group. She was very authoritarian and dictatorial and showed little sympathy or compassion. Instead of an individual, I suddenly, without a shot being fired, had been transformed into a part of a team.

    The walls of each classroom were painted a color that I called "pea green." I guess that color was the most conducive to learning. The floors were hardwood floors, slick and shiny. The ceilings were tall with painted pipes running here and there. The room was cooled in the spring by raising five large windows and heated in winter by two, silver, water heated radiators, that if you got close enough to, you might feel the heat. The hallways smelled of floor sweep that was used to clean them and absorb the dust. The lunchroom was in a separate building that used to be used as part of the Miller School before Grapevine Lake was constructed. It had a smell that I will never forget. One that did not take me long to decide that I wanted to bring my lunch each day except Thursday when we had hamburgers, and sometimes on Friday when fish which always served to preserve the religious beliefs or customs of some of the students.

Mrs. Parr had a long paddle that her husband had made for her, and she wasted no time in demonstrating that she would not be timid in using it. My dad's belt would leave a mark that would soon disappear. But this paddle Mrs. Parr had looked like it could break bones. I didn't want to have anything to do with it. I knew right away that I wanted to be the teacher's pet. She made it clear there would be no "horseplay." One student, named Buddy Slavin, got paddled at least one time every day, and by midterm he was gone, I guess it was his lucky day, because his parents moved away. It sure made a believer of me. I was not about to take any risk with Mrs. Parr's tolerance. I made it through the year not only escaping the taming of the paddle, but also promoted to the second grade, which was taught by Mrs. Dawson. I was glad the year was over.

65. BACK TO SCHOOL AND WILD GEESE

School started after the first of September, to allow the farm boys to help work and harvest the crops on the Grapevine Prairie, but also because we had no air conditioning and usually the weather began to break by this time of year. Soon the patterned flights of geese would fill the sky, and the sounds of their call and the rustling of leaves would signal better times to come.

Still, I never enjoyed the summers coming to an end and having to look at the prospects of returning to school. It meant the barefoot days were over for another nine months. It also meant two new pair of blue jeans and a new pair of shoes. My mother made all my shirts, so they usually were produced during the summer months, or whenever flower sacks were available. Occasionally I did get to accompany my mom to E.J. Lipscomb & Son Dry Goods and help my mother pick out material for new shirts. To say it more accurately, I should say I got to approve the material that my mother thought would go well with my green eyes.

The second grade was not as bad. By now I could read such things as "Go Skip, look at Skip jump." I could recite the alphabet if I tried real hard, and began to develop the handwriting that while unreadable at first, would grow into a thing of beauty during later years. Reading and spelling became the big thing for the next several years.

When I was in the third grade, the most unfair thing happened that I had yet to experience. The principal came in one and day and picked several students out to go to the office where they were double promoted to the fourth grade. I was overlooked for some reason. Looking in the mirror, I decided that it was because I had lost so many baby teeth that I appeared too immature for the fourth grade.

If you were lucky enough to earn the reputation of the "teacher's pet," you gained some special privileges like cleaning the erasers, walking to Main Street to fetch something from a store, or acting as a courier between the classroom and principal's office—cleaning the erasers was a twice-a-year thing. I always was a candidate for the job. We took the erasers out back of the school and beat them on the ground and on the brick walls to get the loose chalk out so they would clean the black board again.

When I was in the fifth grade, Mrs. Robert Stark's room, I was selected to fly the American flag on the flagpole in front of the elementary school. I would put it up in the morning before class began and then select a classmate to help me take it down and fold it properly in the afternoon before school dismissed for the day. I got to become a good friend of the flag and all of its stars and stripes. It was quite an honor to be chosen as "flag boy" and I liked the job even though it meant I had to be at school a little earlier each morning. I got to see a lot of pattern flights of wild geese while putting up the flag that reminded me of the good things that happen in the fall of the year.

William D. Tate

66. RECESS AND SWINGS

The best part of the early school years was recess. An opportunity to drop the shackles and roam free between the swings, the merry go round, and the slides. We would line up and march outside in single file. It was an opportunity to interact with the girls and boys alike. The boys would throw the football or baseball while the girls would jump rope. On bad weather days we stayed in the classroom for recess and played "jacks" or "pickup sticks". The girls were very good at jacks. They tried to teach us how and seemed to enjoy their superiority. Recess was also an opportunity to buy candy at the concession stand set up in the hallway. They had a lot of choices for a penny or nickel. I always looked forward to my candy purchases.

Outside the slides were painted silver and were quite high and a little scary at first. They were fast and a lot of fun. There were just two of them, so we had to take turns. The merry-go round was small and made of wood and painted red, I guess because it was a school color. The boys liked to push the girls round and round as fast as they could until they started screaming. There were two sets of swings totaling eight in all.

The playground equipment was moved around from time to time. First, it was on the south side of the school where we could see it all day if we were prone to look out the window. It was later moved out back of the school and out of sight. When the Grapevine Elementary School was torn down, the play equipment was moved to Heritage Park and continued in use for many years thereafter.

67. WATER FOUNTAINS AND BICYCLE RACKS

There was a time in our community when there were horse troughs along Main Street and a hitching post. The water was for the horses, mules and oxen to drink when they where in town. They were long gone by the time my story began.

Surprisingly, we did not have any community water fountains, except the white, porcelain water fountains that were located in the back of the elementary school and in front of the high school. The water was not cooled by any source, so it varied by the temperature outside. There were some water fountains on the cold drink boxes in some of the stores, including our grocery store. Later, we had water fountains inside that were cooled, and a remarkable achievement, especially on hot days.

Many students rode their bicycles to school, though I never had this freedom. My mother learned to drive and got her driver's license so she could take me to school and pick me up. There were large bicycle racks in front of the elementary school and other ones in front of the high school to accommodate those who traveled by that means. Some locked their bikes and others did not. We had a bigger problem with mischief and trickery than theft. There were no bicycle racks downtown that I can remember. Usually students did not ride their bicycles to town. When they did ride them, they just laid them down in front of the store that they were visiting. They were used more for recreation than transportation. A pursuit of happiness.

68. FAMILY REUNIONS

At one time there were about five generations of my family alive at the same time and living in this area. We had annual reunions both on my mother's side with the Willingham's who almost always met at Grapevine Springs in Coppell, and the Tate family that met at my Great Grandmother Nowlin's residence on Peach Street in Grapevine.

These were great events that usually took place on Saturday or Sunday with a lot of home cooked meals from some of the best cooks in the neighborhood. I remember there was a lot of fried chicken and potato salad and coconut and chocolate pies. These would have been my favorites. There were a lot of little cousins to play with that we didn't get to see every day and a lot of grownups to talk about family stories and good times. Everyone came dressed up and looking nice, especially the women folks. The food would be spread out on a long table. We would get a paper plate and pass by, taking whatever your hearts desired. It was the wait in line that was the killer. There was always iced tea at the end of the line, which you didn't want to overlook because these events were always held in the summertime. After some one said the blessing, quilts were thrown on the ground or card tables assembled for people to sit, while others just set on the front or back porches. After lunch we often explored through the sheds looking at my great-grandfather Will Nowlin's tools. He had a large but old grindstone the family had brought from Tennessee that I like to play with. He came from the old school and measured every move. He was a truth saying, God fearing, Methodist. He was stern and his grandchildren knew not to "cross his path." He was a retired farmer by vocation. It was always a great day for my Great-grandmother Nowlin because she was illiterate and could not read nor write, a great opportunity for her to catch up on family new. There was no limitation on her ability to carry on a conversation. She was industrious and creative. There were not a lot of cameras, back then, and the pictures came out black and white. The highlight of the day was the group and family pictures that have lasted the ages.

The Willingham event at Grapevine Springs gave the boys an opportunity to explore the creeks and dream of the days of settlers and Indians. There was an old water well there where we could throw our pennies in and make a wish. There was always a little water running in the winding springs and it was refreshing to take off our shoes and socks and go wading barefoot after lunch. The men told stories about the family and community, while the women reminisced and exchanged recipes, bragging about each other's favorite dish. The last Willingham reunion that we had there, before so many of the old timers were gone, we produced and distributed the famous Willingham Family Cookbook that preserved the historic family formulas.

The Tate reunions were also done outdoors because Martha Ellen's house was too small to accommodate everyone except those preparing the food. Her house was built around an old log cabin and had a dog run hallway down the middle. Most of the living area was confined to the living room and kitchen. I always enjoyed going in and out of the ornate screen doors that were everywhere. There was a well just outside the kitchen door on the back porch, and I remember being both scared and intrigued when I could steal an opportunity to look down into the well to see how far it was to the water. There was a large elm tree near the street and the men gathered under the shade of this beautiful tree to talk and joke and reminisce.

Martha Ellen was a petite woman who had a good sense of humor. She wore her hair long and put in curls on top of her head. When she was older, she pulled it back straight and wore it in a burn on the back of her head. She often wore her glasses, but also had the a habit of putting them on top of her head and forgetting where she had laid them. She did a lot of handwork, quilting, knitting and cutwork. She had a handmade fly swatter made from a small piece of screen wire on a stick. If a fly landed on anyone, she would swat it, not taking into consideration where it had landed.

She wore a white apron which covered her gingham dresses. She was remembered for her good biscuits. Often there were cold ones on the table that she covered with tea towels. When she got hot cooking, she would wipe the sweat off her brow with her apron. She liked to drink Poly Pop that came in a penny package, and afterwards she would say, "I just can't turn it off." She liked to eat peaches and Hi Ho crackers. She grew up in hard times and did not like to see anyone wasting food. When she was living in a tenant house it burned one night from a faulty flue. After that she did not like to cook at night. She would just fix enough lunch for supper, too,

These events made us all appreciate our families and their heritage in our community, and the inheritance that they would leave us. The last reunion that we had was on Grandma Nowlin's 92nd birthday, which turned out to be her last. We have a great family picture of the Nowlins, Tates, and Stacys taken at that reunion. She was the oldest living member of the First Baptist Church of Grapevine, where she had been a member for 63 years.

When Grandma Nowlin died in 1954, I felt sad. I remember the funeral was in the old pioneer, white frame First Baptist Church on Texas Street, with the bell tower and the prairie architecture. The inside was dark like all of the residences. The bright colored paints had not been developed. It had a wood floor with runners down the aisles. The pews were walnut, the ceiling a cream, colored tin, the walls a neutral wallpaper. There was little color except for the flowers and the stained-glass windows. The baptistry was center behind the choir loft. I realized it was a serious occasion. The days of crawling around under the pews and misbehaving in church were long gone. It was the second time I had been to a funeral in this building, the first being for Mr. Charlie Berry. It was the end of an era that began when my grandmother was a teenager and walked to Texas from Tennessee. After they were established in Texas and three more children were born, her husband Robert Mitchell Tate died at the age of 52 from a heart attack. She remarried, this time to Mr. Will Nowlin, and would find happiness again. Her only daughter, Lura Tate Ratcliff, was killed in a car wreck when she was 40.

Martha Ellen lived a complete life, left fond memories, and is buried beside her first husband Robert Mitchell Tate in the cemetery at Flower Mound.

69. BASKETBALL GOALS

I am not sure when I learned about the game of basketball, but I well remember my introduction to shooting goals in my mother's bedroom which was the middle bedroom. There was a closet door along the south wall. On that closet door, I had a small black rimmed, goal without a net and a small rubber black ball to shoot goals with. This is where I learned to shoot the jump shot one day while I was just horsing around. It was a diversion for me at the time that turned into a crusade or escapade—an exhausting determination to perfect my technique. It became the preferred shot of my time. Every time I am in that room today, my mind goes back to the days of my youth where I spent countless hours shooting goals while my mother sewed or worked in the house. I know it must have driven her crazy for that ball to be bouncing all over her room, but she never complained to me.

When my sister entered junior high, she went out for the basketball team, and I came home from school one day and found our father putting up a regulation basketball goal made from yellow pine with four by four posts. It was set at ten feet, which made it hard for me to get the ball high enough to make a goal, but it was easy for my sister and our father. I watched them and how they shot the ball, and in time as I grew in strength I fell in love with the game and shot goals all the time.

After our parents added on to the house, the basketball goal was moved from the side yard to the back yard and was raised just in front of the old privy that once served as the bathroom. Practice makes perfect, doesn't it? I shot goals several times a week. These were the days that prepared me for junior and senior high school and the opportunity to play on the basketball teams. That basketball goal was one of the best gifts that my father ever gave me.

Oh, there was one unfortunate side effect. We played in the yard and there was always holes or something in the way to trip on. I began to sprain my ankles something that would become a big problem later.

70. MUR'S HOUSE AND HER BABY CHICKS

My grandfather Earl Otto Tate and his wife Myrtle Nowlin Ester Maude Tate lived in the 1000 block of West Wall Street in Grapevine. It had a bar ditch in front, a gravel driveway, and a wooden footbridge along the sidewalk to the house. The yard was planted in shrubs, fruit trees, and flowers of all kinds. There was no grass to mow except the ditch. The house was a white frame house with green trim. It had four bedrooms and one bath, a kitchen, living room, and a large screened in porch in the back and two open porches with two front entrances. The living room was knotty pine and the varnish had turned dark. There was a piano and a couch and chair. Grandmother's bonnet, which she worn when she went outside, hung in the corner of the kitchen. There was a barn, two hen houses and a brooder house, and vegetable garden.

In the spring my Grandad Tate would clean and put up two Martin houses on top of long poles on the fence line next to the garden. Each box had twelve separate bird nests. It didn't take long for the Purple Martins to find their nest each year. Purple Martins are members of the swallow family. The male is a dark blue-purple color which gives them their name. They fly rapidly with a mix of flapping and gliding. They feed high, and catch in mid-air aerial insects like mosquitos, gnats, and dragonflies. Dipping and diving, they were like fighter pilots in the spring. They each eat thousands of insects every year and are very desirable. They like to live in colonies and are attracted by the bird houses. In the fall the boxes were taken down so they wouldn't be invaded by sparrows. I always enjoyed watching these birds flying in the air and raising their young in the Martin houses.

Grandad was short like his mother. He had a round face and was bald headed with a little gray hair around the edges. He wore dentures. He didn't wear any jewelry but he cared a pocket watch in his pants pocket. We called Grandmother Mur, which was short for Myrtle. She was a very pretty girl when she was young, as reflected in her family pictures. She didn't age that well and her face wrinkled. She had the high cheekbones of the Native Americans, but her eyes were a faded blue or gray from her Scottish-Irish descendants. Her hair was the color of parchment. She had false teeth. Her lips were stained by too many years of dipping Garrett Scottish snuff. She was the only person I knew that dipped snuff, but we sold a lot of snuff that came in little tin cans, in the grocery store. Native Americans used snuff before the discovery of America. John Garrett II, who had served as a militiaman in the Revolutionary War, built a snuff mill along Red Clay Creek in Delaware and developed a dry snuff that became popular around the world. I remember each February my grandmother would receive in the mail 100 straight run Buff Orffington baby chicks and would have them in a brooder in her screened in porch.

The brooder was always covered with a quilt to help keep the chicks warm. I could watch for hours as they constantly ate and drank. After a couple of weeks the chicks were placed in a larger brooder and then were transferred again to the brood house where they could be enclosed at night with a light to keep them warm and while they could run and hunt for worms by day. On a Sunday morning in the spring each year, my granddad would bring over three young roosters for Sunday dinner, and he would take three more to each of his other three children. The pullets were put in the pen with the laying hens. I enjoyed visiting the hen house and checking on the laying and setting of eggs.

The family lived primarily in the middle room of the house that was also grandmother's bedroom. There was a butane stove in that room that kept the room warm. On the wall over the stove was the Rexall Calendar that had the zodiac and moon phrases located on it. In this room my parents and uncles and aunts played forty-two and dominos into the late hours on many evenings. In the summertime the living room was opened to receive guest and the front doors were left open for air circulation. I can remember spending the night there with my cousins in the fall and winter months. We would have so many quilts on the bed we could hardly breathe or turn over. It was a cold house.

71. THE OLD IRON BED

I slept in the big iron bed with my father until I graduated from junior high school. It was always painted gold and stood high up off the floor. It was a family heirloom back then, a family inheritance from way back, longer than anyone could remember. All I knew was that it came from my mother's side of the family. It was the bed where my grandfather Bennett died in 1936, the Texas

Centennial year, when he was 62 years old. It was located differently in the room depending on whether it was winter or summer. The room had seven large windows that could be opened during the hot months. These were a disadvantage during the winter when the shades were pulled to try and keep out the cold north wind. The bed had a feather mattress that rested on springs with nice and thin feather pillows. I can remember how the pillows were made. When the young chickens were butchered in the spring for frying, the feathers were picked and cleaned, and then after they dried were used to stuff pillows made of striped duck material especially designed for pillows. Once you have ever slept on one of these feather pillows, then you are hooked for life.

The bed spread hung off the sides of the bed but did not go all the way to the floor. This canopy made a nice place for me to play and to live out my imaginations. It was also a refuse in time of distress. By distress, I mean getting in trouble with my mother, which happened occasionally. The bed will probably stay in the family for many more generations.

72. CIRCUS PONY AND FIGURE EIGHTS:

My father grew up on a farm and logged a lot of hours on the back of a horse, riding to and from school in Lewisville, as well as working on the farm. He would ride to school on Monday mornings and stayed with his Aunt Cora Bonds during the week and ride home on Friday afternoon. It was about a six-mile ride. I heard my father talk about riding horses. Of course, Roy Rogers and my cowboy heroes all had horses, so this made me want one. My dad had a horse in the backyard when I was born, but he got rid of it when I was about three years old. We had a small barn in the lot in the backyard to put another horse. We once had a Duroc hog that I rode like a horse without a saddle or bridle. We always had chickens, laying hens, and a cow, but not a horse.

When I was about twelve, my father went with me to a farm on the corner of FM157 and Highway 183 in Euless to buy a horse. It turned out to be a spotted Shetland pony. When we brought him to our house, he walked a figure eight in the lot. Apparently, he had been a circus pony and walked a figure eight because that is what he continued to do all day long. He wore out a path in the lot that made a perfect figure eight.

He was gentle though and I could ride him. I liked to dress up in my cowboy outfit and six shooters when I rode him. However, one Sunday afternoon, when the horse was tied to a stake in the garden to graze, I got the sudden impulse to crawl upon his back without a saddle or bridle. It was a big mistake. I got bucked off, of course. It hurt my pride but that was all. I had a horse at last.

73. PIG PENS & SHOW HOGS

My first exposure to a hog was at my grandfather Tate's house who fattened a hog with slop every fall. There was something special about that black and white animal that got my attention. I never lost it. It was the New Hampshire breed. The slop bucket stayed in the screened in porch where the leftovers from the family meals were dumped. It got a little strong from time to time, but the pig loved it. My Grandad Tate build a pen each Fall out of railroad ties, stacking them on top of one another until the pen was about 5 feet high. I always wondered how he got the silly pig in and out of the pen without a gate.

We had a pet red duroc hog in the lot in our backyard for a while. I used to get on his back and ride him like a horse, and the pig never seemed to mind. I was never invited to the pig killing but I knew it took place and the results were always obvious. There were big oak trees around town that had the reputation of being hog hanging trees. One was at the old Dorris house on North Main Street. There was a large set of pens and slaughterhouses behind the Methodist Church which were out of sight from the everyday citizen. My father took me there one time and I have never forgotten what I saw. There were two hogs that had been killed, gutted and their hair removed hanging up there. I never had seen such long hogs before and didn't realize they all looked that way when dead and hanging. Farmers used to drive herds of hogs down Main Street to the depot for hauling to the locker plant or slaughterhouses.

Various people had hogs in town back then. Mr. H.V. Yancey had a pen at the bend on Wall Street. Mr. J.H. Wright had sows that ran loose at the basket factory and would go over to the city park to birth their pigs. I remember when the City Marshall recommended to my dad that an ordinance be passed that would eliminate the keeping of hogs in town.

After that we had forty acres out in what is now Southlake and raised duroc hogs there. We got our start from Leroy McCain and Sammy Sparger. I showed a hog at the Fort Worth Junior Livestock show and won a ribbon. I also showed them at the FFA shows in Grapevine that where held on Barton Street. I like to mix shorts, which was a ground wheat, with water, that, stirred together, made slop to feed the hogs. They slurped it down thinking it was the best thing on the farm. One of my top show hogs was named Trudy. I was also involved in the breeding and the delivery of the sows. I had to assist with the birth of a few pigs in my day. We tried to be present when the pigs where born because sometimes the sow needed help having the babies. That was quite an experience raising pigs. We would haul the shoats to the stockyards in Ft. Worth to sell.

74. CURING MEAT AND SMOKE HOUSES

I can remember on a cold Sunday afternoon my father's calling Mr. Bill Shockey who lived off of Whites Chapel Road in Southlake about buying a cured ham. I went with him to Mr. Shockey's place, who had a tall, red smokehouse filled with hams and bacon slabs and shoulders hung on the inside walls. The walls were black from smoke and in the center of the floor were some corn cobs that had been burned to smoke the hams. My father looked over the options and decided on a particular ham and paid Mr. Shockey, and we were on our way home. The next morning, Mother sliced some pieces out of the center of the ham and cooked them for breakfast with biscuits and red gravy. Mother kept the ham in a brown grocery sack in the refrigerator, until finally all of the good cuts were gone and only a soup bone was left.

In a few years my dad started killing hogs at the local locker plant and selling them through the Tate Grocery. We raised most of the hogs ourselves at our farm in what is now Southlake just off Whites Chapel. Dad would bring the hog to the store in the back of his green 1949 pickup truck. The hog's skin would be white after his hair had been boiled and scraped off. There Dad would butcher the hog and sell a lot of it fresh and he would cure the hams, shoulders and sides at my grandfather's place on Wall Street. It was a tin barn with a concrete floor and a wooden bench and walls. It was the perfect place. He would rub the meat with sugar cure and put it in a wooden barrel for a few days. The salt in the sugar cure would cause the meat to drain out the fluids, and then he would hang the meat by bailing wire, to further dry and cure. He would then sell the cured meat at the store. He would cure a new hog every week. Dad would also make sausage out of the scraps and sell the head and feet, usually to a local family. Sometimes he would make country back ribs out of the backbone instead of pork chops. You would cut the back down the center to make pork chops and about three inches on either side of the center to make backbones. The ribs were also sold fresh and usually eaten for breakfast with eggs. The loin was the best part of all. The loin is where that saying "eating high on the hog" came from.

The curing season usually ran from, December through February the coldest months, though the meat would keep for some time in a cool, dark place. Most of the citizens had stopped killing their own hogs and curing their meat and depended on someone like my dad for their supply. He never lost the love of the hog killing and the making of crackling, lard, and sausage. People often had the brains for breakfast the next day with scrambled eggs. I never was invited to indulge in this delicacy, and I am glad I missed out on the bargain. The whole hog was used for something. What was left was mixed together in what was called "scrabbling."

75. QUAIL DOGS AND PICKING PEAS

My dad always had a good quail dog. He had a brass whistle that he used to work his dog. He shot a double barrel Parker shot gun with a pair of pheasants engraved on the receiver. When I was born, Rex, a liver and white English male pointer, was already on the scene. He was a good pet as well as a good hunting dog. He could find the birds and go on point, and he also was an excellent retriever. He loved to hunt and helped pass on the pleasure to me.

There were a lot of quail properties back then, on hedge rows on the Prairie, in the Denton Creek bottoms, and on the timber lands of the Cross timbers. My dad knew where every covey was, and the coveys were back every year. My dad could hunt almost anywhere, but he always went up to the farmer's door and asked for permission again. He never got turned down, but he had to spend some time visiting with the farmer. I remember hunting peanut fields that had been harvested. I could entertain myself by picking up peanuts that were left in the field and eating them raw. I would follow my dad around everywhere hunting the bobwhite. I didn't have any boots, just tennis shoes, and I was always lagging behind because I had to stop to pick out the grass burrs from my shoelaces. Rex lay around in the back yard and was free to go anywhere, but he seldom left the yard unless he was invited. In a moment's notice when given the offer, he would jump up in the cab of my father's pickup truck ready to go. Unfortunately, Dad ran over Rex one day, not knowing that he was asleep under the truck.

The off season for hunting was filled with other things. While the bird dogs whiled away the dog days of summer, we picked black-eyed peas out of the garden and shelled them for Mother to cook for dinner or can. Mother used mason jars to can in the old pressure canner. Many of the locals used number two tin cans instead. I learned how to pick the peas. If you were the one that was also going to have to shell them, you wanted the pea pods to be as mature as possible, perhaps turning a little yellow, because they were easier to shell. You always had to have as few immature pea pods to snap. Picking and shelling was an endless summer task. But the tasty black-eyed peas, with cantaloupe, corn on the cob, fried chicken, and iced tea, was worthy of the labor.

76. CROWS AND MR. CHIVERS

The crow has been part of our society for hundreds of years. Very little value has been placed on them. Who can forget the *ca ca ca* sound of a flock of crows in the fall of the year as they circle around a pecan tree looking for food. Solid black, they look like the first cousins of the raven. The crow pair up in the spring for mating and raising their young, but they flock up and migrate south for the coldest part of winter.

Then on or about 1950 someone invented and started distributing a crow call which looked and operated very much like the traditional duck call. It just had a different sound and mimicked the actual sound of a crow. We could go to the Denton Creek bottom where the lake was being built and get a good hiding place, and when we started calling the crows would start calling back and making their way toward us. They were easy to shoot for those who liked the sport. I still have my dad's crow call.

William D. Tate

The crow was not good to eat, or so was the general feeling about it. Despite the lack of substantial benefit of the crow to mankind, there was little purpose in killing them, unless just to enjoy the sport of shooting something. This first generation of calls was followed by varmint calls and turkey calls.

Charles Wood had some fun with eating crow. There was an African American local named Herman Chivers, who worked for the Chevrolet house. He was a big jokester. Charles had been out shooting crows and asked Herman if he would like to have a mess to eat. Herman asked, "Are crows good to eat?" Charles said, "You bet they are delicious." So, Herman took a brown paper grocery sack full of crows. Charles saw Herman about a week later and he asked him if he had eaten the crows. Herman said, "Mr. Charley, are you right sure that the crow is good to eat?" Charles answered, "Well, you ate them didn't you?" Herman said, "Yeah, but they were so tough you couldn't hardly bite a piece of meat off the bones." Charles had a big laugh, but I am sure it didn't take Mr. Chivers long to get Charles back.

You don't hear much about people hunting crow anymore. But you can use the crow call to attract wild turkey gobblers. Most people use them in that way or have tucked them away in an old drawed somewhere. Back then it was almost a must that you eat what you killed. I would never think about shooting a crow. I bet it is worst than eating a goose.

Mr. Chivers was a fine man. He worked across the street from our grocery store and came over sometimes to get lunch. He would buy a loaf of bread for a nickel and ask that we cut him a slice of boiled ham. One day he came over and made himself a sandwich and looked in the drink case and after a few minutes of pulling up soft drinks out of the ice he said, "All I find is Coca-Cola, Dr. Pepper and Pepsi Cola, don't you have something not quite so strong like a Big Red."

77. CARDBOARD BOXES AND PUPPETS

Just like having wooden boxes to build with, I also had a constant and consistent supply of cardboard boxes out of the stores. I used the big boxes that appliances came in as an initiative to build a scheme of forts and castles to play and hide in. I used the smaller boxes to build all kinds of treasures for my own edification. I would take a medium size box and cut a hole in one side similar to a television screen. I would talk my mother out of a piece of old white sheet to make a screen. It was a hortatory on her part which gave me encouragement to act out my fantasies. Then I would get in the hallway and close the doors. With the aid of a good flashlight, I could create my own show by the use of finger shadows on the screen. Programing for these shows took a lot of forethought. Only your imagination can limit you to the number of creatures and figures that you can create with your fingers if you practice enough.

I had a Howdy Doody puppet that had strings attached like the real one on T.V. I never really learned to use the strings properly to be able to make him talk, but I could move the arms and legs enough to enjoy this toy that I still have somewhere at the house.

There was also a puppet show broadcast on WFAA in Dallas. This was my inspiration to make puppets of my own. A pursuit of cleverness. I took newspaper and soaked it in water and then tore it into small pieces. I added some flour that Mother would provide to me and made a paste. I took the tube inside of bathroom tissue and built a head and a face on one end of the tube. I let it dry and while it was drying, I could work on the face to make them look different for different characters. After they were complete dry, I painted the faces with watercolors and a brush. I then sewed on a dress or pants made with scrapes of material that my mother had discarded and they were cut out and sewn by hand with needle and thread. I had several puppets and wrote scripts for plays and programs that I would perform with the aid of some of my friends. I built a stage out of a cardboard box, of course, that was big enough for us to get behind and be hidden. We experimented and had some great programs that we performed for friends and family. My puppet shows were an escapade or adventure.

78. LEARNING TO FISH

After hearing my Grandfather Tate talk about catfishing and seeing his catch in the sink at the grocery store on spring mornings, I had a hankering to learn the trade. My grandfather caught some big catfish in the Denton Creek. We have some great pictures of him and Oscar Thomas and Max Simmons, who worked in the Grocery Store, with some very large yellow catfish, hanging from a cane pole on the back of my father's green Chevrolet pickup. One weighed about fifty pounds. This got me inspired with the fishing fever. My grandfather did not spend a lot of time with me, teaching me things like that, so I had to depend on my father. I guess I begged my father enough that he finally started to give me instructions.

The lake was not completed then, and our fishing hole on Denton Creek, was a bastille full of catfish. The first thing you had to do was rig your trot lines and poles. We cut willows to make poles with single hooks. They did not have a cork attached but a treble hook and large weight at the end to hold it down. A leader and line with the hook could then be pulled around by the minnow or small perch that was bait. My dad would seine for bait, or we would fish with worms to catch sun perch for bait, fresh every day. Sometimes he would seine in the creek, but most of the time he would seine in farm tanks with permission of the owner, of course. It was important to have fresh bait.

We would go after school and catch the bait or sometimes my father would already have the bait by the time he picked me up at the end of school. We would head towards Denton Creek where the banks were very steep and grown up in sunflowers and cockleburs and other weeds as high as your head. We would set the bait. We also had throw lines or trot lines with several hooks on them that had to be baited. There was a heavy weight on the end, either a rock or old iron that was used to keep the hooks deep enough in the water.

The next morning, we would get up before daylight, after a sleepless night, and head for the creek to run our lines. I was always so excited because we never knew what would be waiting for us when we go to our lines. Sometimes we would have a large fish and sometimes several smaller fish. Sometimes the snapping turtles ate all of our bait and we didn't catch a thing. One time we caught an eel that look like a snake in many ways, but was bigger around and shorter, and had skin like a catfish. I was glad when my dad shook it off the hook and it swam away.

One Saturday morning when we went to run our lines, one of the throw lines was really working with a fish. My dad had to go into the water to retrieve him. The fish was a yellow cat that weighted about twenty-five pounds and was the biggest fish I ever caught in the creek. We brought him to town to show friends as they came in the store and took a few pictures. Later that day my father nailed his head to a tree and skinned him with a pair of pliers and we ate him for supper and for several meals after that. I kept the head and let it dry as a reminder of what you can get when you go fishing.

I remember going with my dad down towards the Carrolton Dam on Denton Creek and walking the bank while my dad fished. He was catching large sand bass that were spawning with almost every cast, and they averaged about one and a half pounds. My dad was a good fisherman. He went to Lake Texhoma and Possum Kingdom Lake regularly and fished for black bass. He took me with him one day to Eagle Mountain Lake though we did not catch many fish that day. I brought bad luck. Dad rented a metal boat from a boat camp and put his 5 hp Evinrude motor on it for trolling. I had to wear a life preserver because I couldn't swim.

My first real fishing trip where I got to hold the pole, however, was at the Austin Patio Ranch Lake. It was a large private lake with a lot of crappie and black bass. We used cane poles and minnows and fished for crappie. This is where I learned to fish and caught my first fish. Sometimes we fished like this a few times on the Bill Crabtree Ranch on Highway 121 that had a lake filled with big fish. Some crappie in that lake weighed over three pounds.

My best fishing trip as a boy was when Mr. A. C. Stone invited me to fish his main lake near his house south of town. He raised catfish and had spawning tanks to breed them. He believed in the chain of life. He raised algae that fed the minnows that fed the catfish. We fished off the dock with a rod and reel. He cut the barb off the hook so it would not hurt the fish because Mr. Stone had a catch and release program. The catfish weighed ten or eleven pounds and were hard for me to reel in. I caught them until I gave out. Mr. Stone cleaned a fish for me to take home to eat. It was the fishing trip of a lifetime for a young boy—an experience that Mr. Stone did not offer many young kids in the community.

79. INTENERATE VETERINARIAN

Even though we were an agricultural community we did not have a veterinarian that received a formal medical training. We had Joe Hicks, who had a ruddy complexion and sandy red hair with a big belly. He wore cowboy boots and khaki pants like a lot of farmers. He lived on Texan street just off Main and had some pens there. He was the person the locals went to for having their dog vaccinated, treating a horse for the Colic or pulling a calf. He was an intenerate veterinarian and the only game in town for many years. He was called Dr. Hicks.

He also liked to fish and was always bringing large catfish to town to show off in the trunk of his car. He appeared to be one of the best fishermen in town, but some of the local men suggested that he telephoned the fish in Denton Creek. That was a process by which you used an old wall telephone with batteries, and you ran wires down into the water and turned the crank on the telephone which sent an electric shocks into the water and caused fish to surface in a dazed condition which would allow a person to scoop them by hand or net. We never knew for sure how he caught so many big fish.

80. OATMEAL BOXES, CRYSTAL SETS AND RADIOS

It seemed in those days before television really got started that the radio was the king for local entertainment. Huley Higgins, Robert Start, B. R. Wall, Paul Barnes and John Hemley used short wave radios to talk with people around the world. Mr. B. R. Wall, a local attorney, carried on conversations with people in the Pitcairn Islands. The rest of us listened to the radio. The news was big, with the likes of Gabriel Heater, but there were programs too, like Amos and Andy, the Lone Ranger, heavyweight boxing championship fights, and such as that. There were a lot of music programs and advertisements. We could get the Early Bird show on WFFA in Dallas every morning. This was a radio show similar to *Good Morning, America* or *The Today Show* now on television. The radio was very exciting to listen to. My dad would come home for lunch and listen to the news on the radio. At night we listened to commentators like Gabriel Heatter who began his show with "there is good news tonight." It was over the radio that I learned that President Franklin D. Roosevelt had died, and that Harry Truman had become President of the United States. I was standing in the sewing room at Dollie Berry's house when we got the word. Everyone was in shock. I remember my dad getting news about the war in Korea and telling me that he might get drafted into the army.

I had an older cousin, Johnny Barnett, who wanted to be a doctor. He liked to mess with radios of all kinds including the short wave variety, and he taught me how to make a crystal set. You took an empty oatmeal box and cut the ends out. You then took a lot of copper wire and wrapped around the box, time and time again as close together as you could get them, until the entire box was covered in copper wire. You then ran a wire antenna to something close to a window. You took a crystal that looked like a piece of lead with a "cat whisker" and you moved the wire around over the crystal, until you could pick up a radio signal. Once you could hear something you would adjust the cat hair until you could hear the voices or music coming over the radio as loud as possible. You had a pair of earphones that you attached to the crystal set that smothered outside noise and allowed you to hear better and more comfortably.

I had my crystal set in my mother's room next to her bed where I could lie on the bed and listen to the radio. I could only get about two stations, WBAP in Ft Worth and WFAA in Dallas. The transmitter towers were just east of Grapevine for the Dallas station, so it was easy to get a signal. It was not as loud as regular radio, but any kid would tell you it was a lot more fun. I really miss my old crystal set, but when I was through with it, my mother put it away to save for me when I grew up.

81. CRAWDADS AND FISHING HOLES

Every boy had a crawfish hole. Mine wasn't much. It was located on Ball Street, just before the bend and before it turned into the Grapevine-Euless Road. The water was usually located on both sides of the street, though neither pool was very big, maybe the size of a small bedroom. The water was usually muddy. The crawdads were grey and came in all sizes. They had two claws that they could pinch you with when you were playing with them.

My dad took me there one Sunday afternoon, armed with a willow pole and cotton string with a piece of fat pork tied on to the string. We were fishing for crawdads of course, which was a great warm up to real fishing. We did not know they were good to boil and eat back then. Sometimes we put them in a big coffee can and brought them home, sometimes we threw them back in the water, and sometimes we used them for catfish bait. When we brought them home and played with them for a while, my dad would take them back to the pond and release them to live another day.

You would just lay the pork bait on the bottom of the pond and wait. The crawdads would not usually jerk like a fish, but sometimes you could see the movement of the line and know to pull it in. The crawfish would be clinging to the pork. We would repeat this for several hours until we either got enough or got tired of fishing and went home. We could see holes around the pond which the crawdads had bored into the ground and stayed when the pond was dry. Then when it rained, they would mysteriously appear again. It was magical.

Too bad we didn't know that they turned red and were good to eat when boiled with corn on the cob, but they are not quite as good as a fried butterfly shrimp basket and homemade French fries from Fagley's restaurant on Northwest Highway.

82. DUCKS AND SUCH

I love poultry and I loved ducks. I was in my fifth year when I learned about ducks as I watched the rubber ducks swimming around my bathtub. Then one year after that someone gave me a couple of colored Easter ducklings that were red and green. I was in the business of raising ducks. I had wanted some baby ducks, but my dad didn't think it was fair to the ducks to dye them. My wish finally came true and they grew up fast, losing their color as their white feathers came in. In just a few weeks the ducks reached their adult size. Believe it or not, I was the proud owner of a pair of Peking ducks.

This meant the next year there would be more baby ducks in the backyard. The duck did not lay in a nest, just on the ground. Dad set the eggs under a setting hen to hatch them. He decided that the adult ducks would be better at a farm. He must have known how fast ducks reproduce so he wanted to cut the supply. They also left a big mess in our backyard and everyone, especially my sister, complained about the problem.

Sure enough, in a few weeks all but two of the duck eggs hatched. They were cute playing in the back yard. I would take the garden hose and make puddles for them to learn to swim and get their backs wet. They would follow their adoptive hen, but she would not go into the mud puddles. Then one Sunday we had some pancakes left over from breakfast, and my mother decided to break off bites and feed them to my baby ducks. We had done this with boiled eggs before and they loved them. She fed the ducklings right off the back porch. This time it was a disaster in the making. When the ducks swallowed the pancakes, they became very thirsty. Then to our disbelief the ducklings started wobbling and falling over and then they started to die, one by one. When they drank water, the pancakes swelled in their little digestive systems and smothered them somehow, and in the end my ducks were all gone.

A few years later I went to the State Fair of Texas with the school choir. There was a nickel game where you throw the nickel and if it landed on top of a plate, you won a baby duck. I won two baby ducks and had them in a little box during the choir performance in the Cotton Bowl. My parents were not very happy when I came home with two ducks.

83. FIREPLACES AND CHIMNEY SWIFTS

The living room had a fireplace in it on the west side. As long as I lived there, we never built a fire in the fireplace because my mother was afraid that it was unsafe. In front of the fireplace was an asbestos cover that clipped into the opening to keep the air and dust from coming down the chimney and into the house. I often would pull the cover back just to explore what was inside. Over the mantel hung two whitetail deer heads my dad had taken on the James River Ranch. On the mantel itself set two Ringneck pheasants Dad had shot near Carthage, South Dakota. On this mantel my sister and I hung our stockings at Christmas time.

The fireplace fit in with the whole room which was dark and dingy. The rug on the floor was old and faded. The pictures on the wall were landscape scenes and the artist had used drab colors. The wallpaper on the wall was kind of a tan, so there was little color in the room. This is the way that rooms were decorated back then. There were no bright colors to cheer the residents up. Yet everything fit in and matched.

My mother later remodeled the room and added some color by painting the walls a moss green and the woodwork a light gray. She threw away the front cover to the fireplace and had the chimney sealed off. She then purchased a set of artificial gas logs that could be burned without threat of fire, and we could then warm and use the room in the winter.

The chimney swifts or chimney sweeps, as I called them, would build their nest in the fireplace in the spring and summer. I could hear the baby birds after they hatched. I liked to open the fireplace to see if I could see them. The nest was usually high up towards the top. I could see the mature chimney sweeps flying around in the air outside. They were dark gray- brown and had slender tube-shaped bodies. They fly rapidly with a constant wing beat. They were so fast I thought they would break the sound barrier. When they fly they give off a high chattering noise. They forge on insects which make them a desirable creature. I always enjoyed hearing the baby chimney swifts and knew they would be back again each year. My dad said they were good to have around because they ate a lot of mosquitoes.

84. PLAYMATES.

One thing missing to this point is any discussion of playmates. There is a reason for that because there weren't very many. My playmate was my sister Sandra for the most part. Most of the boys my age lived in the country too far for me to walk, and my mother did not drive very much to take me. The only kids in range of my age were my cousin Lanny Tate, who lived on Main Street just a half block away and James William Davis, who lived about three blocks west on Ball Street.

I would walk over to see Lanny, or he would come to my house and we would climb on barns and things or play football or baseball or wrestle of just set and talk. It was all about the camaraderie. One day Lanny got stung by an asp at his house that had fallen out of a tree. It was the most painful thing that I had ever seen happen to anyone. After that a big part of what we did was looking out for asp and trying to avoid them.

James William Davis was the son of Ed Davis whom my dad had played football with and who worked with at the Buckner's store. Ed had a dump truck and hauled sand and gravel to customers. He was also a volunteer fireman and his wife was a nurse at Dr. Joe Allison's clinic. He had an older sister named Margaret and a younger brother named Eddie. We played with toys at each other's houses and explored together. He had a pigeon pen where they raised squab to eat. We played with the pigeons some and studied their habits. We played ball some and climbed trees and told stories. I would call him on the phone, or he would call me and arrange a meeting. We had a lot of fun together growing up.

I was invited to a few birthdays. One time I went to a birthday party for Benjamin Huffman out on his dairy farm. They had a big wash tub full of water and red apples floating around. You had to hold your arms behind your back and try to pick up one of the apples with your tongue and teeth. It was very difficult to do. I had never seen anything like that before and my inexperience showed.

At school during recess I got to play with the other kids my age on the swings and merry go round and seesaw. We played just as much with the girls as we did with the boys. On rainy days we played jacks and pick up sticks in the classroom. The lack of regular playmates probably changed my life and made me more of a loner left to entertain myself.

85. GOLDEN BOOKS AND RUDOLPH

Over a course of time my family gave me a series of Little Golden Books, like *Smokey the Bear, Three Little Pigs, Old McDonald had a Farm,* and *Little Red Riding Hood.* Members of my family that were well educated with college degrees thought it was important to learn to read at an early time. I inherited other such books from my big sister, Sandra. They were all kept in the bookcase on the west side of the living room and readily available to me when I had the desire to read. I used to like to go through these books often and pick out a couple to read though I had read them so much I knew them by heart. I can remember, before I started to school, I would sit in my mother's lap and listen to her read these stories to me.

I loved these old books, especially the one called *Rudolph*. This was a great story. There was no Rudolph when I was born. He came to life a few years later. He was an unusual reindeer because he had a very bright red nose that shown when it was cloudy, dark or foggy. It was a great story because children have to learn that you can overcome some limitations that you are born with like Rudolph was able to do. Since my dad went deer hunting each fall, there was a lot of talk in the house about deer so I fell in love with this particular story. There was also a song about the same story that was sung by Gene Autry. I still have an old phonograph record of it and the lessons it taught.

I would take the Rudolph book off of the shelf often, and used it even in the summertime. I never got tired of it. It seemed so real and practical. I also like the times when it snowed. I had never been to Colorado or some state where it snowed a lot. My experience with snow was when it snowed in Grapevine, which didn't occur very often. The thought of snow added a lot to the story and was refreshing to read on a hot summer day when the temperature was over 100 degrees. I never got tired of it and of the lesson it taught. This and several other children's book from that time are still sold in stores today.

I had another old Christmas book I liked to read. Santa Claus had red fuzzy clothes on for the cover and on each page inside. We had an animal book and other children story books that I read often. Some of these same books are still sold in stores, are all classics.

86. FIRECRACKERS AND ROMAN CANDLES

We sold firecrackers in the grocery store before they became a more tightly regulated product. They were popular only at Christmas time because we normally did not celebrate the 4th of July unless it was a private family affair. Santa Claus usually filled our stockings with fireworks, and it became a tradition on Christmas night to get together in the yard or a safe place to have a fireworks display. We usually used the west side of the yard, next to Church Street to set off our Roman Candles and bottle rockets.

There were no formal fireworks displays in Grapevine back then, so the private use of fireworks was a big part of Christmas. I guess we were all careful because I don't remember anyone's getting hurt or setting a neighbor's yard on fire. It was usually cold on Christmas Night so we didn't last too long, out in the cold, setting the fireworks off.

The firecrackers came in flat pads of 25, 50 or l00 each. You could play with them yourself without supervision. All you needed was a match or lighter. Then there were Roman candles, which were long tubes; you would light one end and hold it in your hand. There would be ten or fifteen separate shots come out of the canister a few seconds apart and sometimes would be different colors. They would explode in the air. They were more typical of modern firework displays but much, much smaller. Then there was the rocket, which was on a long wooden stick. The firecracker itself looked like a small rocket. You would stick the stick in the ground and light the rocket. It would take off sending the rocket, stick and all skyward and then it would explode in the air.

There were red chasers, which were about a half inch around and about six inches long. When they were lit, they went crazy, circling in unpredictable directions just above the ground. It would make us kids, jump, run and dance around trying to avoid the chasing firecracker. There were also bottle rockets which were like small Roman candles which you put the stick in a Coke bottle, light and it would take off out of the bottle, shot into the sky and explode. There were all kinds of other fireworks. One was shaped like a small airplane that we could launch. There were other fireworks that would explode with a loud boom and others that would explode in the air in an aerial display. The best fireworks of all were the sparklers which came twelve to a box. We lit them with a match, and they would send sparks flying everywhere. We would usually do it at night and twirl the sparkler around in a circle. We were allowed to do the sparklers by ourselves because they were not dangerous and would not set anything on fire.

87. BIRTHDAY CAKES AND MEASLES

When I was a kid, we didn't have a birthday party every year. I can only remember one big party which my classmates and friends were invited to bring presents. I was ten years old. My mother made me a cake that looked like a merry-go-round with animals lined up around the cake. The party was at my house on the afternoon of my actual birthday. It was always important to celebrate your birthday on the actual day regardless of the day of the week it fell. My friends all brought me nice presents. We played games, like hide and seek, jacks, walk-on- stilts, and held sack races. Then we would blow out the candles, sing the happy birthday song and cut the cake. It was just like Christmas in May.

My mother invited Judy Stinson, a young girl that she thought I might be interested in, and took several pictures of me and her and the cake. It did not work out though. Judy was the smartest girl in the class and even then was focused on what she wanted to be in life.

I enjoyed my tenth birthday so much I talked my mother in letting me have another one when I was twelve years old. I looked forward to it very much and my mother made the cake and worked hard to make it a perfect day for me. But when I woke up that morning, I had come down with the measles and my party had to be cancelled. I never had another childhood birthday party. I think it is good that kids get to experience a party every year during their childhood. It is truly the most special day of the year.

I think that my mother just could not bear to throw birthday parties for me because it was just a sad time for her, a reminder of losing my baby brother who was born just one day shy of mine. Or maybe kids just didn't have birthday celebrations back then because I cannot remember my sister having a birthday party either, other than a cake with the family.

88. MUFFINS, HOT ROLLS AND COOKIE JARS

My mother had many talents. She loved music and she loved to entertain. She loved to teach and she loved to be involved in the Methodist Church and Eastern Star. The family remembers her best for her cooking, especially her homemade hot rolls.

In the old house on College Street where I grew up, the kitchen was on the northwest corner of the house with a back door and two big windows on the west. It was cold in the winter and hot in the summer. We did not have central heat and air. Opening the windows was the best way to circulate the air and get a fresh breath of oxygen. Cooking only added to the temperature problem. My mother never complained. She would make large white cake muffins. There were twelve to the pan. I loved to eat these muffins just as they came out of the oven. Mother did not put icing on them, so we ate them plain. She also made a lot of cookies, cakes, pies and cobblers. We had an antique cookie jar that had been handed down from previous generations. Brown with hand painted yellow flowers on the side, this is where the cookies went, and I had full access. The cookie jar sat on a cart that was in the corner of the kitchen and I could access the jar easily without mother knowing it. I ate a lot of cookies. The jar is still in the family though I broke the lid.

My mother made ice box fruitcakes for Christmas. She ground up graham crackers with a rolling pin and mixed in small marshmallows, candy fruit, pecans, and molasses. She then poured it in a cake pan and put it in the refrigerator to set up After a few days it was ready to cut and boy was it good eating.

She also made homemade yeast rolls for special occasions such as Thanksgiving and Christmas. She mixed the flour with yeast that used to come in about a one-and-a-half-inch square. Somehow the yeast mixed with the flour and when allowed to set, it would rise into dough. Mother would put a wet towel over the bowl during this phase of the process. After the dough had risen, she would put just the right amount into each of the cups, in the same pan that mother baked muffins. They would rise and when baked came out of the oven golden brown. They would just melt in your mouth with a little butter. Everyone raved about the fresh rolls and looked forward to the special dinners.

89. HOUSE FIRES AND MAKING KITES.

I always wondered what you used a fireplace for if you never built a fire. I had not been introduced to campfires and roasting hot dogs yet. I did like to back up to a stove and get the seat of my pans as hot as I could get them without catching them afire. Our house was cold in the winter, so we stayed in our bedrooms where we had natural gas heaters to keep the house warm though we turned them off when we went to bed. My dad had had a couple of houses burn, from faulty flues when he was growing up and so we did not burn fires at night. We were afraid of fires.

My dad did not make a lot of toys for me, but I remember one in particular that he did help make was a kite. I had never heard of a kite. Dad got a couple of small pieces of wood that were about three feet long and two foot long respectively. He then used old newspaper and wallpaper glue to fold over the sticks and make the kite where it would catch the air. It was not very colorful or pretty, but it worked just the same. He had a roll of light string to tie to the boards where they crossed in the middle. We went out to the country where there was plenty of space to fly the kite. At first it was hard to get the kite in the air, and once there it wanted to do a nose-dive. My dad decided the kite needed a tail, so we went back home to invade mother's sewing rags to make a long tail out of cloth pieces to give it a tail that would give it some balance so it would stay in the air. It worked. I enjoyed the kite on many occasions, mainly on Sunday afternoon when the stores were closed, and the family was hungry to have something exciting to do.

90. BY THE OUNCE OR BY THE POUND:

I learned very early in life how to wait on customers in the stores. "Can I help you, sir?" "Yes, I would like to buy some seed." When someone came in, I directed them to where the particular item they were interested in was kept. I would show them what we had to offer. In the spring everyone in town and in the countryside planted a garden so this was a busy time of the year for us. We had a small scale with a large brass tray on top to weight the small seed by the ounce. There was a scale with the numbers 1 through 8 on it which represented ounces. If you wanted to weigh one ounce you would put the weight on 1. If you wanted to weight over one-half pound, then you had round weights you added eight oz. of weights to the end of the scale. The seed were kept in a large wooden cabinet which had a picture of the plant on the front of each drawer and the name of the product. People bought Iceberg lettuce, Danvers half long carrots, Detroit red beets, Purple Top turnips, Florida Broadleaf mustard or Curly mustard greens, Bloomsdale spinach, Icicle radish or red top, crooked or Early Prolific Straightneck yellow squash and white squash, Straight Eight or Boston Pickling cucumber, Clemson Spineless Okra, and various varieties of tomato seed by the ounce or half ounce. We put the seed in a small brown bag and wrote on it the kind of seed and the amount to be paid. Some seed might be 15 cents an ounce while others might be 35 cents an ounce.

Customers also purchased corn, beans, peas and potatoes by the pound. We had a larger white scale that we measured these items by the pound. These seeds were kept in a large, oak cabinet or in bags on the floor. We had several kinds of English peas, black eyes, purple hull, crowder peas, and several kinds of corn. Golden Bantam was the most popular, but we also had Iroquois white corn and Yellow Dent, both considered field corns. Alaskan Early and Wando were popular English peas which had to be planted early. Our supply of beans, included pinto beans, Yellow Wax beans, Burpee Stringless Green Pod, Contender, Provider, Tendergreen. Kentucky Wonder was a pole green bean that was often planted to run on the corn stalks. There was Fordhook, a white lima bean and Henderson specked lima beans. Another speckled lima was a pole bean called Jackson Wonder that was planted on picket fences or trellises.

Irish potatoes and onions were the first things planted. February 14 was the popular date for planting these. We had both the Kennebec white and Pontiac red potatoes. You cut the potatoes up in chucks with an eye in each that would sprout and make a plant. They planted white potatoes in the black soil and red potatoes in the red sands. We also had package seed that people could buy; however, buying in bulk per punce gave you more seed for your money. We sold white Bermuda onion plants and yellow hybrid as well as a variety of pepper and tomato plants in individual containers. Mr. Jess Hall went to the Texas Valley every spring to buy Homestead Tomato plants to plant in his fields and always sold a few to us to resell to the public. They were sorted, 50 plants to a bunch, and wrapped in newspaper. They were kept in a number three wash tub with a small amount of water in it to keep the roots moist. You had to water them for a couple of days after planting to get them growing. We did not sell flower seed in bulk, just in pre-filled packages.

91. EXTERMINATORS AND FLOOR SWEEP

During store hours we left the front and back doors open for ventilation since we had no air conditioner other than a large ceiling fan in the grocery and a swamp cooler in the hardware. At one time there were large screen doors on the building, but they were removed. This meant that a lot of dust that was stirred up on Main Street found its way into the store, both on the floor and covering the merchandise which had to be constantly dusted with a turkey feather duster.

We had pine wood floors covered in the aisles with a black rubber mat. To keep them clean, we spread floor sweep that was nothing more than sawdust which had a red oil base added. It had a distinct smell to it that was very pleasant and was something we had in a 25-gallon drum purchased from a Mr. Madison, who was also the exterminator. I would use a scoop to take the floor sweep out of the barrel and spread it lightly on the floor and let it set for about fifteen minutes to dispense oil upon the floor, and I then would begin sweeping it up and throw it in the trash. He came around periodically, usually on a Saturday to exterminate in various areas of the store to kill crickets, ants and other bugs that might t appear. He wore khaki shirts as well as pants and wore a hat. I always looked forward to seeing him. We paid him by the month to perform these jobs. He lived in Denton and had a 100 acre farm at Tioga where he raised some cattle.

92. BUMBLE BEE AND ARKANSAS VACATION

We did not take many summer vacations. When we did it was usually to the Texas Hill country to see the deer. One year there was an exception. My dad wanted to take us to Arkansas and Eureka Springs to bathe in the healing hot waters. The day we were leaving, I was walking around in the back yard out by the vitex trees and I felt a sharp pain in my instep on my right foot. Looking down I saw a bumble bee setting on my foot stinging me. It really hurt but I was afraid to say anything to my parents or my sister for fear they would cancel the trip. I did not know that vitex trees attracted bumble bees. The vitex tree had purple, white, and pink flowers on them all summer long. I later discovered that the vitex trees which I climbed and played in so much were an important flowering tree for the beekeepers and are a significant summer honey flower.

Getting back to the story that night after we checked in to one of those old fashioned small, separate building, shabby motels, I was taking a shower and my mother noticed that my foot was swollen to twice its size. Upon inquiry I had to spill the beans and tell her the truth. My dad had to find a drug store that would open and sell us some Epson Salt to soak my foot in to get the swelling down. It did work, but I still could not get my shoe on, and it affected my enjoyment of the trip. I learned a good lesson about telling the truth and not hiding things from my parents. I was also very careful in the future walking in the grass in that area afraid I would get stung again. I can remember one time at my Granddad Tate's house that my granddad and dad got into a hive of bumble bees and fought them with paddles. This also happened one time at the barn in our backyard. Fighting bumble bees was a childhood pastime for my dad and granddad. I heard they often fought them until their eyes were swollen shut from all the stings. I never wanted to have anything to do with bumble bees after I got stung. I sure didn't want that pain and experience again. Strike me off the list of bumble bee fighters.

93. FOOTBALL GAMES AND HOMECOMING

I remember the old football field where Faith Christian Middle School now sits. It had a native rock wall around part of it and posts with a wire through them to keep cars from driving onto the field. The bleachers were handmade of wood. The field ran north and south. The players' locker rooms were in the old grade school gym, and the players walked back to the lockers after the game accompanied by family and supporters. There were some great games played there with stars like Herbie Hodges and Leonard Gifford. When the new high school was built, a new field was built that had new metal bleachers to go with the old homemade ones, equally divided between the home and visitor's sides of the field. I can remember how cold I got at the football games. Our parents had warm, wool clothes that they had before he war, but the kids' clothes were made mostly from cotton the war effort having taken up all of the wool cloth. I would get so cold my teeth would chatter.

We had some great football teams in the early '50s with stars like Jerry Pair, Leon Baze, Sherman Milner, Richard Jackson, Hal Nelson, Jack Howard, Leonard Gifford, Junior Tate, Jerrell Estill, and Freddie Cates. I looked up to these guys and wanted to grow up to be like them. They won several district championships but always got beat in bi-district when they had to play the teams from oil and gas fields of West Texas. I can remember from my house on College Street, I could hear Skipper Chaffin on the public address system calling the game on a cool, fall Friday night. The game had to be stopped about 9 o'clock for the freight train headed east caused so much noise until it passed, the players could not hear the referee's whistle.

The homecoming was always special each year. High school classes started weeks before making floats for the parade. It was a great time of comradery for the students even though the senior float almost always won first place. Having former students who had moved away who came back for homecoming was always good. The day itself was exciting with a pep rally before school was out and then the homecoming parade down Main Street let by the Tarrant County Sheriff's posse on horseback carrying the American and Texas flags. Then we had hot dogs and chili at the old school cafeteria. Years later a homecoming dinner on Saturday night became traditional. I still have the homecoming ticket to the meal on my senior year in high school. The game was not always against an easy foe, sometimes we were even playing for the district championship.

94. FIRST AND SECOND DEER HUNT.

My first deer hunt was on the Ernest Geistweldt Ranch in Mason County, Texas. It was a day lease. We paid $10.00 a day per gun to hunt. We stayed in a one room red barn with a wood stove in it. We unrolled our sleeping bags on the wood floor. My Granddad Tate went along. One year he did not want to go but I begged him, and he agreed to go. He had been having some health issues. I was only eleven years old and did not understand such things. What would happen on this trip was the beginning of one of the worst periods of my life.

I was excited of course. I had watched my dad and granddad prepare and go deer hunting for years and I could not wait to go myself. We often went to the hill county for a weekend in the summer and looked for deer, so I knew what they looked like and how hard they were to see in the brush. We saw a few does but no bucks. As for me I loved going out and climbing up in a tree to look for deer.

When we came in from the morning hunt the first Saturday morning, my granddad was in bed. He had a heart problem that had not been addressed.

It worried me of course. We soon realized my granddad did not need to be there so we went home early Sunday morning. My granddad went to the doctor the next week and was diagnosed as having heart problems and was placed on nitro pills to open his arteries when he was having chest pain. He only lived a year after that, dying of a heart attack just before deer season would open the next year in 1956.

We took his place that year on the Ruben Schnieder Ranch in Gillespie County. We had met at Abe Statum's filling station, a few days before to plan the trip. We left on November 15, before daylight and drove to the ranch, stopping on the way for breakfast in Cleburne. We were staying in a camper that one of the hunters had rented, sleeping in a bed over the kitchen table. The wind blew all night and rocked the trailer. I don't think I ever went to sleep because I was so excited. The ranch was in the big red granite country not far from the famous Enchanted Rock. My dad and I hunted together on a large rock overlooking a creek and I got a shot at a five-point buck. I shot his tail off but did not kill the deer. Mr. Coats who was hunting down the creek killed the deer when he passed by. I fell in love with deer hunting, a past time I would follow all of the days of my life but would go for five more years before I killed my first buck.

95. THE BASKET FACTORY

The Grapevine Basket Factory was owned and operated by J.H. Wright at 601 W. Wall Street, Grapevine, Texas. There was a red plank barn down by the creek that had one side open that housed the machinery. They cut large cotton wood trees that were abundant in the area, along the streams, and laved then in to eight inch logs about two feet long, for trimming into stripes. The thin strips were then used for making handle and bushel baskets and during World War II, they also made egg crate for the war effort. Over the years a lot of cotton wood trees disappeared from the area including those along Grapevine Creek the site of the peace treaty.

I past by the basket factory every time I went to visit my grandparent Tate's. The baskets were used by local truck farmers to carry their produce and they often sold the tomato's, cucumbers, squash and cantaloupes by the basket rather than by the pound. A lot of citizens had gardens and we sold some of those baskets in the store for them to use in their own harvest. Mr. Wright's son, Lemoine Wright was cutting a cotton wood tree for the factory one day and the tree fell on him and killed him, leaving a widow, Mattie Mae Wright and a son Joe Wright and a daughter Jean Wright. The grandparent Wrights had a sow that ran loose on the farmstead, and one day she came up with a litter of pigs and Joe asked his grandmother where the pigs came from and his grandmother said the sow had gone down to the creek and must have found the liter down there. Then Joe went down to the creek that afternoon looking to see if he could find more pigs.

96. THE BACHELOR

Oscar E. Thomas never married and never had any children. He was a lifetime bachelor and what some called an ole maid schoolteacher. He taught at Coppell and coached tennis. He lived on the property that he owned on Main and College. There was a large, two-story house and he lived upstairs. There were two apartments downstairs, one occupied by the Stadiums who had two daughters and Mrs. Bartley, a seamstress. Mr. Thomas was a slender man with white thinning hair. He was a complex person that lived a simple life. He was very frugal which allowed him to assemble his investments. His upstairs was cluttered with a collection of books, magazines and newspapers. He did not have a television but read a lot. There was a green metal bed and a couple of chairs for furniture and a hot plate for coffee. He dressed modestly with slacks and a white shirt. He wore no plaid or color, except his tie on Sunday. He drove a Chevrolet, but walked to town and the Methodist Church on Sunday just a block away. Even into the eighties he would drive to TCU or NTSC and play tennis with the girls on the tennis teams. He liked to shoot pool and play dominos at the recreation center on Main Street. He also liked to hunt and fish. He fished in Denton Creek for catfish and hunted deer with my Granddad Tate in Gillespie County, Texas. They caught some large catfish in the creek before Grapevine Lake was built. When in deer camp if you didn't eat all he cooked then he would cut back on what he cooked the next day. They used tin cups and plates and he would make his fellow hunters wipe their plates with the blue tissue paper that came wrapped around apples before they put them in the pan to wash. He hunted deer with an old 30.30 rifle and wore knee high leather boots. He liked to creep hunt which was crawling on hands and knees and quietly moving from brush to tree not to spook the animals. It was a procedure that I would adopt myself in later years. Mr. Thomas also liked to hunt for arrowheads in the Denton Creek bottoms and found a lot of arrow points from the native tribes that lived or hunted here. He was one of our town's most memorable characters and I learned a lot from him growing up.

97. PEANUTS AND CRACKER JACKS

Growing up in my Granddad Tate and father's stores gave me a lot of options and exposed me to a lot of things that other kids my age did not experience. We had three stores: a grocery store, a hardware and a furniture store. My Granddad Tate was a butcher in the grocery store, so I spent a lot of time there in my earlier years. The grocery store is where my dad put me to work dusting merchandise when I was 6 years old.

In the middle of the grocery there was a long candy case made of oak wood. It had glass on three sides and doors on the back to get to the candy. It was also open on half the top where customers could reach in and retrieve candy. We had all kinds of candy including peanuts and Cracker Jacks. These were some of my favorites not only because they were delicious but because they had prizes in them. I was easy to fall for all kinds of prizes. We also had a similar case where the bulk and box candies were sold by weight. Some of these were seasonal, especially at Christmas time. I remember the smells that came from the bulk candies.

Redskin Spanish peanuts came in little round red boxes that were larger than a quarter but smaller than a half dollar. They were about 2 1/2 inches long. They had a round lid on each end that could be opened. The box of peanuts cost a nickel. They came in a case of twenty-four. The peanuts were good to eat dry or to pour in a bottle of Coca-Cola. Boy were they tasty. The salt on the peanuts made the Coke spew. Sometimes the box of peanuts would have a prize inside, usually a nickel which meant if you were lucky enough to get a box that had a prize, you got the peanuts for free. Since I was working in my father's grocery, when no one was looking I used to take the boxes of peanuts and shake them to try and tell which box had the prize inside.

On the other hand, there was the box of Cracker Jacks that were in the same kind of box that they have always been in, rectangle, with the words written on the side, " Cracker Jacks." They too had prizes inside, not all of them, but only the lucky ones. I used to shake the boxes of peanuts and Cracker Jacks to see if I could hear a trinket inside. It was hard to do, but after all I had the run of the whole case. Still, it was mostly just the luck of the draw. Sometimes I got lucky but most of the time I was disappointed.

You always got to eat the peanuts or Cracker Jacks so prize or no prize there were no losers. But none of the other candies held a mystery like that. You bought candy just for the candy and that made it worth the price. That was enough if you were buying a Babe Ruth or a Hershey or Almond Joy.

98. CHEERIOS & SHREDDED WHEAT

One of the great discoveries in my life was the breakfast cereals. The major manufactures were General Mills, Post and Kellogg's. Wheaties was the Breakfast of Champions, but I never did care for them that much. They were always promoted by star athletes with their picture on the box. I was more attracted to the products that captured the attention of small boys through surprises that I could find inside. But to get Mother to buy the cereal to have a chance at the prize I had to eat the cereal, so it had to be something tasty as well as palatable. My dad liked Post Toasties and 40% Bran Flakes so I learned to like both of them. But, my favorite was Cheerios, which were loaded with surprises. You could get all kinds of things like license plates for your bicycle or a key chain. Some had coupons where you could order things like six shooter belts with holsters and cowboy outfits. Sometimes you could get a wooden airplane that you put together and could fly. Other times you might get a balloon or a small figurine. Whatever the manufacture put in the box just mean they had to put in less cereal.

I learned to eat Shredded Wheat that was akin to learning how to eat dry hay, but if you mixed in a banana or some strawberries for flavor, it was pretty good to have every once in a while. They came in little compressed bales that even look like hay. You pulled them apart and suddenly your bowl was full of cereal before you even put the milk in. As time passed many more delicious cereals were developed and put on the market. Rice Krispies, Puffed Wheat, and Wheat Chex's. Since I grew up in a grocery store, I knew immediately when these new products hit the market and always wanted to try something new. However, if it offered a prize, then that was even more good fortune. We took eating cereal by spells. Sometimes we had it for dinner instead of breakfast, but most of the time it was breakfast during the summer. I had a hard time learning how to say breakfast, calling it "breaksus" instead. People would laugh and make fun. For the most part my mother got up early and cooked a good breakfast of bacon, sausage, and eggs, biscuits and gravy. There were always leftovers still in the oven when I got home from school.

99. SWIMMING HOLES

When I was growing up in the community, we had no swimming pool and individuals did not have them in their back yards. In earlier days there had been a nature spring and big hole that made a pond where locals went to swim. It was located just off of Dove Road a few hundred feet north of Northwest Highway.

As a result of lack of facilities, I didn't learn to swim as a boy. The farm boys on the prairie had stock tanks to learn to swim. I heard a lot of stories from people who said their dad 's just threw them into the tanks or creeks, and they would have to swim to get out. There were no formal lessons, no one teaching swimming. It has been one of my greatest regrets. Dad would take us to Ft Worth to Sylvania Pool on Belknap Street once or twice a year. Growing up on a farm, he was a good swimmer, but he did not have the patience to teach me though he gave it a try now and them. I did not like to get my head down in the water and the splashing got water in my nose. I learned later that I had a rather unusually small nasal passage, and it was difficult for me to breath in the water. I probably would never had been able to learn to swim.

When I was about ten years old Grapevine Lake opened, and there was plenty of swimming opportunities. However, we had watched the lake being built and knew about all of the gravel pits that were left around the lake. For the first ten to fifteen years at least ten people drowned each year in the lake, so we didn't dare go there swimming, ever. I did see my dad, one cold winter day when we were duck hunting around the Grapevine Lake, go into the water to retrieve a big greenhead mallard that he had knocked down. I also saw him go into the water to retrieve a fish that he had hung on a trot line or cane poll. I was scared of the water, so those experiences frightened me.

100. THE SECRET ROOM

Everybody has a fantasy or a special dream that they dream time and time again. As I began to mature, my parents added a room on to our house that we called the den. It was made from knotty pine just like the living room of my Granddad Tate's home. It attached on to the back bedroom where I slept and grew up. There was a hallway leading to the den with a bathroom on the left and closets on the right. The first closet was my dad's and the second one was mine. In between there was a suit closet and some drawers for underwear and socks. This room would become my bedroom with a small bed among the deer heads, books and pheasants that decorated the wall and symbolized my life. In the summertime I could look out the east window and see the moon and the stars just like I had been able to do in the old bedroom when I was a small child. It was very pleasant and there on many nights I dreamed and contemplated what God's plan for me might be. I dreamed big. It was here that I made the decision that I wanted to be an attorney when I grew up like one Texas famed defense attorney, Dusty Rhodes.

I often had a dream in those days and for many years later about a secret room behind the closets in the hallway. I dreamed that one day I discovered in the back of my dad's closet a hidden door that I opened. Behind the door was a secret room filled with toys that I had always wanted but never had. I went into the room and played for hours. I decided that it would remain my secret. I never told my parents or my sister of its existence or anyone else before now. I would return many nights when I was bored, and my parents were asleep to open the door and play in my secret room until I was either satisfied or I had to return to my bed before dawn so I would not be discovered.

101. SHOWS AT WILL ROGERS

When my sister and I were still pretty small our parents wanted to expose us to the big live shows, like Ice Capades, that came to Will Rogers Coliseum in the 1940s. It was a traveling entertainment show featuring theatrical ice-skating performances. They had some former Olympian skaters who had a lot of talent and put on a colorful show, with bright costumes and dazzling exhibitions. I was amazed at how they could skate in circles and even backwards.

We also went to see the Ft Worth Rodeo and Fat Stock Show. We walked around the barns and exhibits and looked at the livestock being shown by FFA and 4H boys and girls. Then we headed for the big building with the round roof. A cameraman who took our picture and gave us a number, but we didn't buy. Inside, the seats were steep and high which giving us a good view of the cowboys and the bucking stock that they rode. I liked the bull dogging the best. A cowboy jumps off a running horse on to a long horn steer and wrestles it to the ground. The fastest time was the winner. I remember the smell of sweat and animal poop as well.

But the best of all was the night we went to see the Greatest Show on Earth, the Ringling Bros. and Barnum & Bailey Circus. It was billed as three rings under the big top, and it was all of that. They did have three rings or circles and there was some performance going on in each at all times. There were ladies who climbed ropes to the top of the building and swung on swings and jumped and were caught by men from swings who were performing with them. Then there were the elephants and their majesty. There were dogs, bears, and animals of all kinds that could do tricks that most animals could not do. At the end they brought the lions into a wire cage in the center of the stadium. We were very close. We could see the lions come in from long chutes that led to a big cage. It had a lot of benches for the lions to sit or stand on. The lion tamer was a man who had a long whip that kept the lions in check and a safe distant from him. The show was spectacular. I couldn't help but be a little uneasy wondering if one of the lions could escape and what would happen to me if it did.

102. DRESSING UP WAS HARD TO DO

Growing up with an older sister in a time with little to do except make believe and play acting and homemade toys, I was called upon to do some things that you would not have expected me to do. As boyish as I was and strong willed too, you would not have thought that my sister could talk me into dressing up with her. It was a flumadiddle or what you might call utter nonsense. But what is even more alarming is that my parents thought that it was unique or perhaps "cute" enough to take a few pictures that have lined the family picture albums ever since. As I grew up, I looked up to my sister for guidance and to lead me into the adult world. She achieved that for me for which I am grateful. But I am glad that this dressing up was a passing fancy and didn't become a part of a regular routine. Yes, I put on women's clothing that was too big for me, whether it came from my sister's closet or my mother's or both. The pictures tell the story. I remember that everyone saw it as fun, without the political or culture connotations that might be suggested later. In addition to the wardrobe, there were the high heel shoes, bobby pins and curlers in the hair, and, of course, the makeup that made the part look authentic if not a little silly. I wanted to leave this chapter in my life out of the story, but I had promised myself when I started that I would tell the good, the bad, and the indifferent. As I would have it, it turned out to be just make believe.

103. POST OFFICE AND COMIC BOOKS

My father's and grandfather's stores were in the 400 block of Main Street on the west side and just as few buildings down from the U. S. Post Office and the City Drug Store. Part of my job was to retrieve the mail. Grapevine was a central post office that served customers for miles around by rural routes. We had a post office box in the post office, box 125. It had a combination that I must have opened a million times. They put up the mail all day long as it came in, so we had to keep checking the mailbox all day. The post office was a big square room with a hardwood floor and a couple of desks for addressing and stamping mail. There was more than one customer window, but usually only one was open and it was adequate. You could look through this window and see the bags of mail piled on the floor and the employees at work sorting and preparing the mail. Sometimes baby chickens arrived through the mail and you could hear them making that baby chick sound in the back. Sometimes I ordered quail eggs through the mail for hatching and I was always excited when they arrived. When you received a package, they put a note in your box to go to the window and make claim. Mrs. Sue Mullins was the Post Mistress.

Next to the post office was City Drug, a very inviting place for a kid. Besides all of the medicine there were all kinds of cosmetics and gift items and smells of various sorts. There was a large soda fountain where pretty girls poured up fountain drinks or strawberry ice cream sodas. You could also buy hand packed ice cream in square white boxes for take home. It was better than the commercial ice cream Cabell's or Vandergriff's that you could get in the store. I think they handled Borden's ice cream at the drug store. Borden's also produced milk and delivered it to your front door. This was a real treat on a hot summer day.

But even more inviting at City Drug, was the comic section and magazine rack where I could go and browse through the pages. It was located in the north front corner of the drugstore next to one of the large front store windows. I was a regular customer. I bought a lot of comic books, especially if there was a new Tom and Jerry or Donald Duck, but I thumbed through even more that I bought. I would read them over and over. I wished my mother had saved those old comic books instead of throwing them away.

104. OUR SUMMER BEDROOM

The coming of summer not only meant off with the shoes but also brought about a change in our sleeping habits. Our house did not have air conditioning. Instead it had dry fans that were placed in front of water dripping window units to bring about some break in the day and night heat. This is why people built their houses with dog runs or screened in porches in earlier times. The dog run was as open space or long enclosed hallway down the center of the house to allow for air circulation.

We stayed up late and slept late in the morning. We soon would move our mattresses to a bed in the front side yard and would lie outside after dark, watching the stars, fireflies, and barn owls. The neighborhood was dark, so the neighbors could not see what we were doing though they knew we were there. We were the only ones in town that did this as far as I know. My dad and I would have a good conversation about various things: about life, our past, our hopes and our dreams for the future, and what was going on at the stores or in town. We talked about what happened that day, about history, current events, government, and school. We talked about the farmer's crops. We talked about the construction of the lake and about catfishing in Denton Creek. My dad told me about the family and how life was when he was growing up on the farms in Denton County. He told me how much hard work it was to sickle hay and put in the shock and to follow a mule all day and keep the rows straight. He told me that they grew most of what they ate, so they always had plenty to eat but never much money. He told me to respect money and how to manage it. He talked about the two fires that destroyed their farm homes and about the fire that Grandmother Nowlin had when they were living on the Cluck Place. He talked about how generous neighbors had been in replacing furniture and how important it was to help people in need. He told me that everyone needs a little help sometime in their lives. He told me to always be generous to others and that they would be there for me when I needed help myself. He told me life was unforgiving, that when you made a mistake, you were not always given a second chance. He told me to always tell the truth and I would not have to remember what I had said. Sometimes we would be so engaged in conversation we didn't realize that the day had ended and that the darkness had pushed the burnt orange sky beneath the horizon. We would then research and study the stars and locate the movement of Orion, the North Star, the Big and Little Dipper, Venus, and the Milky Way. This outdoor sleeping practice was not suitable for my mother and sister and they never participated. It was a boy thing. The air would cool off during the night and we would have to pull a sheet up over us.

Then at first light we would move inside, or at least I did and my dad would go to work. I would lie as close as possible to the evaporated cooling unit and would sleep comfortably until about 9 o'clock. This made me a night person instead of a morning person. I still like to stay up late at night and sleep as late as I can in the morning. Habits are hard to break.

105. CHICKEN, PORK AND A SIDEOF BEEF

I often travelled with my father to Ft. Worth and Dallas to get supplies and merchandise for the stores. One of the things I will never forget is going to Ft. Worth to the poultry processing plant. It had big doors opening to the street so I could see the whole process. They would take a white feathered chicken out of a coup and hang it upside down on hooks along a conveyor belt. The chicken would be de-headed, then moved to the plucking machine. After being fully processed, they would put the dressed chicken in a wooden crate filled with fresh ice. There would be fifty fryers to a box, which is usually what we bought for the weekend at the grocery.

One time 200 baby white leghorn roosters came into the post office and no one claimed them so my dad bought them. We raised them in the back yard and then processed them. We did not have a plucking machine, so we skinned them. We started selling them when they were small fryers so we could get rid of them in four weeks before they got too big. We only did this once. My dad also raised hogs on the 40-acre farm we had west of town. We had a locker plant in town that my dad would take a hog to be slaughtered and processed. When dad would picked up the hog he would put butcher paper in the back of the old green Chevrolet pickup, and lay the hog on top, and take it to the store where he butchered it. He would sometimes buy a side of beef and take it to Jetton's in Ft. Worth and have the whole side barbecued and sell it in the store as a special. Most of the time he would buy a hind quarter and front quarter of beef to butcher and sell as steak and roast. We often cut the beef individually for a customer who wanted a certain cut and a certain thickness.

106. RADIOS AND TELEVISIONS

Everyone always had a radio or two growing up. We not only listened to the news but to programs like Amos and Andy and the Lone Ranger, or to boxing matches and sporting events and murder mysteries. I remember how exciting it was to listen to the heavyweight boxing championships. The announcers made the match very vivid and thrilling. This is what we did at night for entertainment. My dad had a radio in his room by his bed, and I often sat in the bedroom and listened with him. I made a crystal set that I have written about elsewhere which I listened to the Early Bird Show in Dallas WFAA and also music. Yes, music on KLIF was where I learned to appreciate music.

Then in the early '50s when I was about 10 years old, the T.V. arrived. They came in wooden cases with screens of 10, 12, or 14 inches. We were some of the first to sell them in town in the stores. We brought one home, of course, and my grandparents got one too. It was not long that everyone wanted one. There were only a couple of stations-to-stations to start with, WBAP Channel 5 in Ft. Worth and WFAA Channel 8 in Dallas. They did not have programs all day and night, just certain times. They had things like Mr. Rogers, and Howdy Doody time and, of course, the news and weather. When they were not programing, they had a symbol for you to tune the TV. Then came the Lone Ranger and Hopalong Cassidy and much more. There was boxing on Saturday night sponsored by Pabst Blue Ribbon beer. Then you could watch pro football on Sunday. The featured team broadcasting to our area was the Cleveland Browns. Otto Graham was their quarterback. The pictures were all black and white. Before colored television you could buy a plastic cover for the screen, which was blue at the top, red in the middle, and green at the bottom. It added some color to the programming but was nothing like the movies that were in color. You had to have an antenna on the roof or in the attic to get good reception. I remember that we had a tall antenna attached to our chimney above our living room for many years. Everyone knew if you had a television if you had an antenna on the roof. Later when the towers got stronger, you could get a set of "rabbit ears," as they called them, that was a small antenna on the TV. This would give good reception. The television was the biggest invention to come after World War II and revolutionized life in America with shows like American Band Stand and the Ed Sullivan Show.

107. FLOURSACKS AND BINS

In the grocery store when I was a kid, we had large mahogany bins with large draws. In these bins we kept bulk sugar, brown sugar, salt, pinto beans, lima beans, and other products. We sold them by the pound or half pound. We had metal scoops that we used to put the products into brown paper bags and then taped the top so they would not spill. Above the bins we displayed all kinds of detergents and soaps.

At that time flour came in cloth sacks. They came in 5, 10, and 25 pound bags. The bags were made of pretty cloth and housewives collected them and made aprons, dish towels, dresses, shirts and other clothes from them. During the war and after cloth products were not very plentiful and this was a way to help promote and sell the flour. My mother made me several shirts from flour sacks.

108. VACATION BIBLE SCHOOL

Every summer for a week we had Vacation Bible School at the church. It never failed. It was a big deal. The church bell rang, reminding everyone to come to Bible School. Every morning we went to class down in the basement of the church building where the Sunday school rooms were located and heard stories about different characters in the Bible. Sometimes we had pictures to color in reference to the lesson. Then we would break for games and refreshments. We played baseball, badminton, hopscotch, pop the whip, and etc. My dad would ice down soft drinks in a number 2 wash tub and donate them to the kids. It was, of course, very hot in the summer and the cold drinks really hit the spot. The sponsors would make homemade cookies that were really good. The food and games were the incentives to get kids to want to come.

We put together a program to be performed on the Sunday following Vacation Bible School to show off for our parents. We would act out some play or story in the Bible and dress up like the characters in that story. The parents always thought it was cute. I felt a little self-conscious about it but looking back it was fun to act out the stories of the Bible.

William D. Tate

109. PARADES AND CARNIVALS

The big parade, and the only parade we had each year was the homecoming parade. It was led by the Tarrant County Mounted Sheriffs Posse, who carried the American and Texas flags and was followed by the fire trucks and many horses. It became such a big event we even started making class floats that were judged with prizes awarded. We worked on the floats for a month before homecoming, which added a lot of anticipation to the event. Attendants were selected to ride on the floats by each class. The floats and the homecoming queen nominees were presented at half time of the football game and the winners announced.

We only had one high school, so everyone was an alumnus and looked forward to this weekend. The parade on Friday after school was followed by the football game that night and a homecoming dinner that usually was hot dogs and a lot of gossip.

Each summer a carnival came to town. Some years the circus came under the big top and some years it was just the carnival or maybe the skating rink would come for a week or two. This was our summer entertainment. You could throw balls and if you knocked all of the milk jars off you got a prize. I like to try this because you could win if you played several times. There was a merry go round and a Ferris Wheel. The Ferris Wheel was a little too scary for me because it went as high as the trees and always stopped when you were on top and rocked you back and forth.

The carnival was set up on Barton Street on the west side of the stores on Main Street. This lot is where the political rallies were held in election years. All of the candidates would come out on a Saturday night and meet people along Main Street. They handed out campaign buttons, nail files, and campaign matches with the candidate's name printed on it, so you would remember to vote for them. The lot was also where the FFA boys from the high school would have their annual livestock show. It was one day even held on a Saturday in May. The farm boys would build temporary pens to house the animals that would be judged with ribbons presented. The men of the town, many farmers themselves, liked to do their own judging and admiring the well-kept animals. The next day the pens would be gone. Just some scattered hay and manure would be left as evidence that it even happened.

My Barefoot Days

110. HARRIS HATCHERY AND BABY CHICKS.

I went with my father a lot to Ft. Worth to get supplies. The route left Grapevine down Hwy 121 which turned to Belknap in Ft. Worth. At the intersection of Beach and Belknap on the north side of the road was Harris Hatchery. Every time we passed that way, I noticed the hatchery and always wondered what was inside. We had chickens in the back yard and always had plenty of setting hens to raise all of the baby chicks I could ever want, but I just wanted to stop at the hatchery to see what was inside. I am sure I pestered my dad every time we pasted by to get him to stop, and I am sure he ignored me because he knew what I knew that we didn't need any more baby chicks.

But one day my dad stopped, and I final got to go inside. The hatchery had big incubators and several breeds of baby chicks. They were so many of them and so fluffy, I was all eyes. My dad did the choosing and we got to buy a dozen Rhode Island Reds, which seemed to be his favorite breed and brought them home in a box with holes in the side to let air in for the babies. We put the chicks under a setting hen that had no eggs and put them in a portable well house that had been built for Sandra and me to play in. There I watched my chicks grow up.

In the years that followed every time we passed by, I wanted to stop again but I didn't have to imagine anymore what was inside. I knew. This is where I fell in love with incubators and hatching baby chicks..

At Easter time the feed store had white leghorn baby chicks that were dyed greens, blue, red, and purple for Easter. I always wanted to raise some Easter chicks but my dad did not like the dying and selling of chicks like this. He would never buy me any because he said they would all grow up to be white leghorn roosters that no one had much use for them except to eat.

111. RELEASING FISH & BOAT BUILDING

When Lake Grapevine was announced, I was too small to realize the impact on our community. I was at the groundbreaking ceremony and I had experienced firsthand the importance of Denton Creek for fishing, especially catfishing. We went to the construction site almost every Sunday to watch the building of the dam and the removal of trees and gravel from the lakebed. My Uncle Dick Wiley was president of the Fort Worth Anglers Club during this period, he was instrumental in getting the State Fish Hatchery at Eagle Mountain Lake to begin stocking the new lake with game fish long before it was a lake.

I remember the day that a white truck pulled up in front of the hardware store to get my father to go to Denton Creek to begin the fish stocking program. Of course, I had to tag along. We drove down to an area that had good access to the creek at the Murrell Bridge. The truck had twelve large baskets of small finger long black bass and crappie kept alive by a air pump. We took these baskets and turned them upside down dumping the contents in the creek. This process was repeated several times that spring before the dam was completed. Channel catfish were also stocked in the lake. After the gates were closed impounding the lake, fishing was closed for two years to allow the small fish to grow up. By the time fishing was opened at the lake, the black bass weighted 1 1/2 to 2 pounds each and were a very nice catch.

In anticipation of things to come, my dad bought a wooden, flat bottom boat kit and assembled the boat in the furniture store across the street from the hardware store. After it was put together, it had to be sanded and then it was covered with fiberglass and a fiberglass cloth to protect the wood. It was clear when dried so the boat had a natural color. Dad bought a trailer to carry it on and for many years, stored it back of our house. I remember every time it rained, I had to take a coffee can and dip the water out of the boat and the vitex leaves that it collected. My dad had a 5 hp Evinrude out board motor than he had used to fish Texhoma and Lake Dallas and Eagle Mountain Lake with for years. It was a good trolling motor, which is the way we fished for the black bass with various colors of Bomber artificial lures. The white with red head and the white with a black jagged line down the side were the most effective. Every time we trolled down an old roadbed or crossed one, we would get a bite. This was before "catch and release" so the fish made a good meal for dinner.

112. CANDLE LIGHTING & MISTLETOE

The big event in our community for Christmas each year before we became the Christmas Capital of Texas was the Candle Lighting Service at the First Methodist Church directed by Ms. Madeline Hemley. Volunteers started decorating the sanctuary a week before, cutting cedar in the countryside and cutting down mistletoe from the trees in town which were loaded, especially in the prevalent hackberry trees. We took cane fish poles to poke the mistletoe down from high in the trees. It was a blessing to the trees because mistletoe is an invader that damages the trees over a course of time. The white berries were on the mistletoe this time of the year and gave off another fragrance to the Christmas season. The mistletoe was mixed with the cedar to provide cover for the candles that lined the window seals and along the railings of the church. These candles would be lit early in the program as the sky turned dark outside, giving a feeling of the Christmas Star inside.

On the Sunday afternoon of the service, the church would be filled. Each guest would be given a candle that would be lit towards the end of the program and the church bells would be rung. Christmas songs were sung and the story of Christmas and the birth of Jesus told. The service always ended with the singing of Silent Night and the lighting of the individual candles. Then the guests would file out of the church one by one and their candle extinguished by attendants at the back of the church. It was good to get us in the Christmas spirit much like the Carol of Lights has done in more modern times. There is one similarity. That is after either one, Christmas seems to come very fast each year.

113. THE BIG SCARE

As I have said before, in those days people used home remedies a lot to treat themselves for medical issues of a minor nature. My dad had a sore throat one night and decided to gargle some salt water, which is not a procedure that I was familiar with and never tried. It might have been an old-fashioned home remedy. I usually got the distasteful, red cough syrup when I had a sore throat.

Dad got strangled on the salt water and it closed up his esophagus and he could not breathe or talk. I did not know what was going on, as he came out of his bedroom. He was obviously in great distress. He was choking and appeared to be suffocating. He was making a loud noise trying to breathe and was walking around making a terrible sound as air was trying to enter and be exhaled. My mother, sister and I were scared to death. I could see concern in my dad's eyes as well. It was a cold winter night, but he went outside, trying to get some air, and I followed him. He continued to try to breathe and was making such a loud noise a neighbor came over to see what the problem was. I was afraid he was going to collapse and die at any moment. I did not know whether he was having a heart attack or what. I did not know what to do. I did not know about the Heimlich Maneuver or how to do the abdominal thrusts at the time. He was apparently getting enough air to keep himself alive, but I did not know this. Finally, he started getting a little better and was able to breathe in more air. But it seemed like it went on forever.

Soon after our neighbor came, dad was able to talk again and tell us what had happened. We called Dr. Joe Allison who came to the house to check him out. I remember him being there with his black medicine bag. After examining my dad, he told us dad was alright and it was just salt water that strangled him. I was so relieved to know that we had nothing to worry about, but I thought it was a close call. It still scares me every time I swallow something the wrong way and get choked.

114. CITY SERVICES AND FIRE TRUCKS

The City Hall was on Main Street, almost across from our hardware store. On the south side was an office where we paid city taxes and water bills at the City Secretary's desk. City Council meetings were held in this part of the building. A couple of card tables were set up for each meeting. On the north side of the building was the Library. It had shelves all around the walls filled with a lot of old books. Most of them were classics instead of novels. The building had no air conditioning and a gas stove for heat in the winter. The floors throughout the building were unpainted concrete. It was dark and dingy, the way you would expect a library to look like back then.

In the back of the city offices and library, fire trucks were stored, and the firemen met and kept their equipment. On the north wall of this back room was the city jail. It was a cage made out of 1 inch flat iron welded together with a door on one end. It had a cot or two inside for sleeping, but no bathroom facilities except a chamber pot. There was no heating or air condition, of course. The night watchman tried to get the prisoners turned loose before morning, so the city would not have to buy them a meal. Prisoners were usually ones who had a little too much to drink and only needed to sleep it off anyway. The back of the building had doors raised with ropes to allow the fire trucks to exit. As the city grew it had to store some of the fire trucks out back of the building. The fire facilities served the volunteer fire department that had served the community from its beginning, starting with the bucket brigade, that met regularly and fought fire with whatever they had.

115. BAPTISMS AND WATER MOCCASINS

My parents belonged to the Methodist church which has a practice of baptizing by sprinkling young babies so their lives would be dedicated to be raised in a Christian environment. This event occurred when I was just a few weeks old, and my mother made me a special dress for the occasion. Later when you reach the age of accountability, you have to make the decision to be baptized again by sprinkling or immersion for the forgiveness of your sins.

Some churches like the Baptists, believe that you should be immersed in water, like Christ for your sins to be totally washed away. My dad's family was Presbyterian and a member of the Flower Mound church until they moved to Grapevine. My dad told me about being baptized by immersion after a camp meeting one summer when several young people were baptized in Denton Creek. The only problem with creek baptisms was that there were a lot of water moccasins that lived in the creek. Anyone who knew very much about water moccasins knew that they were an aggressive snake and would come after you. They were also poisonous. The girls were all afraid of the thoughts of snakes and were reluctant to go into the water, so the minister had some parents armed with rocks or pistols who were on watch and prepared to scare away any snake that might appear during the ceremony. This was sufficient security for girls. I hated snakes and I was also very self-conscious. I was embarrassed just by the thought of the attention I would generate by being baptized, and I certainly was not going to expose my body to the likes of a snake.

William D. Tate

When I reached the age of accountability, my mother patiently waited for me to make that personal decision.

116 COTTON SACKS AND BRACEROS

Grapevine was a prairie town. It was a cotton town. Every year the First National Bank gave a prize for the first bale. The harvest came in late August and the Mexican Braceros came to town to pick the cotton by hand. The partnership between Mexico and the United States was created in the 1940s because farm workers were in short supply, especially in the southwest United States, because so many American men had enlisted in the military to fight the war in Europe. The word "bracero" means "those that labor with their arms." They usually had one- to six-month contracts to work in the states. After the crops were all harvested, they then returned to Mexico with their money. I thought it was a good program at the time for the cotton farmers on the Grapevine Prairie. Merchants downtown sold cotton sacks. They were made of white cotton ducking material. They came in eight, ten, twelve, and fourteen feet lengths. They all had a strap that went across your shoulder. You had to be strong enough to pull the cotton sack down the rows until you got to the end of the row. Children used the shorter sacks and grown men the larger ones. The women also picked cotton, which was really picking bolls. You would reach into the plant and pull the bolls off the plant and put them in the sack and then pull the sack along to the next plant. You picked two rows at a time. You got paid two cents a pound. When you go to the end of the row with as much cotton as you had the strength to pull then you weighed out, dumped the cotton in a trailer and started over. The farmer kept a tablet how much you had picked and paid you at the end of the day.

Cotton sacks were hung up outside stores in the fall together with sugar cane that was available this same time of the year. Sometimes the stores also sold pumpkins if there was a local farmer who raised them that year. It was the signs of fall and the blessings of harvesting another crop and another year. It meant the farmer could pay off his mortgage and have cash to pay his bills for the rest of the year. It was an exciting time to see the cotton trailers come to town to the gin and to see the 500-lb. bales of cotton sitting in the yard of the gin or on the platform at the depot to be shipped by rail to the textile mills.

The road from the Grapevine Prairie to the Gin on Church Street in Grapevine, past by our house, and in the Fall of the year, the edge of the street along College and Church Streets were white with cotton that had fallen off the trailers.

117 BANANA STALKS AND OTHER FRUITS

I can remember when bananas came on stalks just like they had grown. We had a hook in the grocery store where we hung the stalk. There was a knife nearby, stuck in the post, to cut off how many bananas that you wanted to buy. They came in a little green but ripened fast in the Texas air. We did not get bananas all year long because they did not keep in the hot weather. One time when we went to San Antonio on vacation, we saw the banana trees growing there, but these were more ornamental than eating bananas. It was the first time that I had ever seen a banana tree. Most table bananas were imported from Mexico or South America, picked green, and then kept cool until they were ready to sell. Pineapples were not in season, except one time of the year. They had to be flown in from South America. Apples keep a along, time sitting on the cellar floor, and so we had them all year long. Citrus fruits like lemons and limes we had most of the year because they grew in California and Florida as well as the Texas valley. We had oranges most of the year, but the real good Texas navel oranges we only had at Christmas time. We had the white grapefruit most of the year, but the Ruby Red Texas grapefruits we only had in the cooler months. Table grapes from California were available in the fall. Strawberries were available in the spring. Avocados were not available in North Texas but were grown along the Texas border. As a kid I had not been introduced to the words "guacamole" or "salsa."

118. MASON JARS AND TIN CANS

Nearly everyone had a big garden back then which means they grew a lot more than what they could eat fresh. Deep freezes eventually came along so vegetables could be frozen, but before that the only home remedy was canning.

William D. Tate

Canning came by two means, either by the jar or by the can. If by the jar there were two main brands in Texas, the Mason Jar Company or the Kerr Jar Company. They seemed to me to be very similar other than the name molded in the glass. We handled both varieties at the same time in the stores. Buying was a question of habit rather than preference. They both came in several sizes with twelve to the box; the most popular ones were the pint or quart. Number two tin cans came two dozen to the case. We only sold them by the case. They were smaller than a pint. You had to have a sealer to put the lid on and seal it. You turned the handle and it sealed the can very tight before it was brought to high press and preserved. The glass cans required a pressure cooker or canner. They were cooked under high pressure before they were sealed tight. They would last for several years. Some people stored the cans or jars on shelves in out buildings while other kept them in cellars if they had one. The cellars were cooler, and the canned vegetables lasted longer but the cellars sometimes seeped water and ruined the cans. We sold these jars and cans by the hundreds of cases during canning season, with everything from corn to peas to beans to beets, carrots and okra being canned. Usually, cabbage was made into sauerkraut in a large crock jar that was allowed to age and ferment. The kraut could be canned into the glass jars but was usually kept in the crock until it was empty. The gardens and the vegetables everyone produced is why there were so many good cooks.

119. CHARGE ACCOUNTS AND COUNTER CHECKS

In the grocery store and hardware our regular customers had charge accounts. Sometimes people could not pay, and I think my father often gave them credit knowing that he would lose it. We were an agricultural town and the farmers had money at times during the years while at other times their money was invested in their crops, fertilizers, and insecticides. We had a double walnut case that had metal sheets that raised or lowered and on each sheet were several spring clips that held individual accounts. Our charge tickets were about three by five inches and were filled out for each visit. Then they were assorted and placed in each person's account. They were then summarized and added up at the end of the month. We normally did not send statements in the grocery store; customers came in when they wanted to pay up. In the hardware store we did it alphabetically and sent monthly statements. Most of these customers paid monthly after billing.

People did not have personalized checks. They used counter checks that were printed by the banks. For most of my youth we only had the First National Bank of Grapevine. The checks were printed with orange or yellow ink. They had the bank routing number but not the individual bank account numbers on them. The bank sorted them by customer and debited their account. It made it easy for people to write checks. Later it became more complicated with electronic technology and all of the problems created with fraud and theft. Of course, most people paid cash for their purchases either in currency or by check. The customer would just fill out the amount and sign their name and the check would be honored. This was before plastic credit cards, which revolutionized the industry. It was a hard but simpler time when money was hard to come by for everyone.

120. QUAIL PICKING AND CHURNING

My dad used to like to quail hunt. There were a lot of quail each year on the Grapevine Prairie and in the Cross Timbers. My dad used a 20 ga. L.C. Smith shotgun and had an English pointer bird dog named Rex. My dad would always drive up to the farmhouse to talk with the farmer to get permission to hunt, which was always granted after a little visiting. My dad was a good shot and I followed him around and spent most of my time picking grass burrs out of the shoe laches in my tennis shoes. Oftentimes Granddad Tate also quail hunted but never with my father. He used a 20 ga automatic shotgun. When I was old enough to graduate from a bb gun my dad bought me a single shot 410 which I could use in hunting dove but not quail.

I can remember dad bringing in quail after dark on fall and winter evenings. He would leave his hunting vest in the kitchen until after dinner, and then I would get a brown paper grocery sack and start skinning the quail rather than picking them. For some unknown reason we always picked the dove, but we skinned the quail. I remember how the quail had a wild smell to them, and even worse when you cleaned out their insides. They sure were good eating though when fried and served with biscuits and gravy and maybe some English peas.

The kitchen was a workshop for the family. I remember my mother churning in the old crock churn that we still have in the kitchen. It was hard work. She let me take turns in raising and lowing the dasher. We always seemed to have a milk cow that my dad milked before he went to work and at night after dinner. We put the milk in pitchers in the refrigerator to separate the cream from the milk. The cream would rise, and we would churn it to make butter, then place it in molds to cure and set up. When pasteurized milk and butter came along, it was much healthier to eat and cook with. The milk cow was sold and we no longer churned or made butter. We just brought it home as needed from the store.

121. GRANDDAD TATE AND CHERRY SPRINGS

My Granddad Tate, like my father, enjoyed going hunting and fishing. He got this desire, growing upon on the farm as part of the duty to provide food for the table. My dad did not hunt with his father or fish either. I never knew why. Granddad hunted deer on the Reuben Schnieder Ranch near Cherry Springs, Texas in Gillespie County in the heart of the Texas Hill Country. It was about a 1,000-acre ranch and had two camp sites on it. One was a concrete and rock garage with a wood cook stove, hutch, table, and concrete floor. The hunters brought their own cots for sleeping. It had an outhouse out back. A couple hundred feet south there was a tin barn with a concrete floor used by other hunters in the party. My granddad stayed in the concrete house with Oscar Thomas, Bob Thwcatt, and Ira E. Coats. They usually hunted four or five days on the opening of the deer season, when they got their deer. They did not go back. My grand dad was not a trophy hunter and usually killed small bucks. There were a few wild turkey's but not many were ever killed. You had to shoot a buck bigger than a spike. It had to have a forked point off the main beam that was long enough to hold a washer. My granddad shot a buck one day that only had a start of a point, and he was caught with his pocketknife trying to carve the horn enough where it would hold a ring and be legal. On another hunt Granddad shot a buck and climbed down out of his tree stand to process the deer. After he straddled the deer, it started to come to life. He got his rope around his antlers, and they went around and around tearing up the grass and brush as they struggled. Granddad finally got the rope tied to a tree where he could get to his gun and dispatch the wounded deer. A lot of interesting tales came out of deer camp.

122. FILING STATIONS AND FIXING FLATS

There were several filling stations not far from where I grew up. Abe Statum had a Gulf station on the corner of Main and College, and Ted Willhoite had a Texaco station at the Corner or Main and Franklin. They both sold gas and fixed flats. The Gulf station had an outdoor ramp that you drove your vehicle upon to have the oil changed. The Texaco had an indoor ramp that was raise hydraulically. They both fixed flats out in front of the store. The Texaco also sold and fixed large tractor tires. It was not unusual for someone to drive his tractor to town to get a new tire or get one repaired.

The Gulf station had a large bor d' arc tree out back that stood over a barrel to disposed of their used oil cans. In the area around the station, which also served as a drive through, they periodically spread out shredded shingles that had been taken off roofs. The shingle material got hot in the summer and melted and stuck together. In a way this was better than gravel. A kerosene tank and pump stood next to the front of the building and a cold drink box on the other side. When you opened a bottle drink, the cap went into a container that you removed and emptied when it got full. These bottlecaps were scattered around the building also to help lay the dust. They had a facility where they washed and polished cars. It was just four metal pipes, one in each corner, with a roof, a concrete floor, and a drain from the floor into the sewer. They washed cars by hand with a water hose and a large sponge. Inside they had a checker game going all the time. There were tires on the racks to be sold and cans of oil for sale. Mr. Stadium also had small deer horns from deer he had killed in South Texas mounted on the walls. He had taken the hair off the skulls and polished them until they were ivory colored. The door to the men's rest room was on the inside while the door to the ladies had an outside entry.

Willhoite's was a much bigger store. It also sold appliances and repaired vehicles. It was a Goodyear dealer. One time they had a promotion offering coupons for gas purchases to buy various brown plates and dishes. I got my mother an entire set of these dishes that she used on special occasions.

There were other filling stations, especially along Northwest Highway, that sold gas and repaired vehicles. Slim Chambers had a garage underneath the Grapevine Masonic Lodge. Bart Starr had a filling station in a native sandstone building on the corner of Main and Northwest Highway. The Dalton Bros had a Sinclair filing station on Main Street where the Gazebo is presently located. These types of business, including a Western Auto Store that sold tires, became very prevalent after the arrival of the automobile.

123. SATURDAY AFTERNOON MATINEES

Farmers came to town on Saturday, making it was the biggest and most popular day of the week. The stores were closed on Sunday and people went to church and worshiped. Drawing for prizes happened in the early afternoon for the grown-ups, while most of the kids went to the matinee at the Palace Theater. It was always a double feature on Saturday afternoon for the price of one and took up the whole afternoon if you stayed for both. One was always a western, plus there were always the cartoon and advertisements. There was a concession stand stood inside the front door where you could buy popcorn and a drink and all kinds of candy. The balcony was closed except when there was a large crowd. Mr. W. A. Guest ran the place and didn't allow any horseplay or smooching. He walked around with a flashlight making sure that was no vandalism going on or any hanky-panky with the young lovers. It was a great way to spend the afternoon when your parents had other things to do. The movie cost 25 cents and I would usually walked from the stores and watched for a while. Then if I got tired or bored, I left. Sometimes I would just watch the western movie and leave after it was over.

124. DONKEY BALL GAMES & GLOBE TROTTERS

In the late forties and the early fifties people in small towns like ours depended on the traveling entertainers to bring some life and joy to the community. We have talked about the circus, the skating rink and the carnivals that came to town, usually in the summer months. But what about the winter when the days were dark and cold? We had our high school girls and boys basketball teams, of course, that played to a full house. Other entertainment came to town not every year but once in awhile. One was the donkey ball game. There was a troop who had a team of donkeys that were gentle enough for anybody to ride. They came to town in an old bus that was converted to a donkey trailer marked, "Donkey Ballgame" I can remember them coming to town a couple of times and playing in the old high school gym. Some businessmen in town would ride the donkeys, and they played the boys high school team. You would have to ride your donkey and shoot your shots off them. Of course, you had to dribble, and you would have to dismount to gather a loose ball. It made for an interesting game. They put rubber shoes on the donkeys so they would not hurt the hardwood floor. A couple of years later the school district refinished the floor on the gym and didn't let the donkey's come back to play. The donkey basketball game always played to a full and screaming house as everybody rooted for their favorite team.

The Harlem Globe Trotters were world famous even back then, but they played at a lot of small places, and not just the big stages like Madison Square Gardens. They played the high school basketball team one year again to a full house of people who were hungry for some new entertainment. The Globe Trotters were tricksters. They were all they were advertised to be and much more. They were unbelievably skilled and, of course, they won easily over the less experienced team. They brought their own referees and played by different rules. The game was the talk of the town for a long time.

125. WOMANLESS WEDDING AND CAKE WALKS

The churches used to be the center of activity in the community, especially the First Baptist and the First Methodist where I went just down the street from our house. There was the Candle Lighting Service at Christmas, the Christmas Tree on Christmas Week, the Revivals for a week in the summertime, Vacation Bible School, and a trip to church camp near Glen Rose.

One summer I guess there was a need for a fundraiser for a local project, I am not for sure. The idea was to perform a womanless wedding. This was not a novel ideas, a script was available that others had performed. It was the thought itself that was novel. There was a bride alright. But of the characters were men regardless of their role. The men of the church acted and starred in the play which was produced by the music director Madeline Hemley. It was performed only once on a Saturday night in a stage set up in front of Leach Hall outside; chairs were set up for the patrons. A lot of still pictures were taken to remember the event. A.J. Harper was the bride dressed in a gown with makeup and a veil. Gordon Tate, my father, was in the play, as well as Ed Davis, Floyd Deacon, Earl Deacon, and other local businessmen. Yes, it got a lot of laughs and was one of those events you never forget.

There were other fundraisers at school for the PTA, like spaghetti dinners, bazaars, and fall festivals. One of the things that made money was the cake walk that was held at almost every event. The mothers made cakes to raffle off. There would be chairs in a circle. It took a quarter to be in the game. The emcee would hold up a cake that was to be the prize for each event. They tried to fill all twelve seats before the music would start. This meant four dollars a cake which was a lot of money when a loaf of bread was selling for a nickel. When the music stopped, you set down. There was a number under the cake. If you were setting in the chair that had the same number, t then you won the cake. My mother was a very good cake maker and usually had a cake in the event. It was not about having a cake to eat, it was all about winning.

126. VALENTINE BOX AND EASTER EGG HUNT

The only time we had a valentine box was when I was in the second grade, and Mrs. Gertrude Dawson was my teacher. We celebrated Valentine's Day in several grades but not with a valentine box. My mother and father helped build the valentine box out of a cardboard box that a Christmas wreath had come in. We covered it in red crape paper with white valentines cut out and glued to the sides of the box. There was a slit in the top of the box like a mail drop. I took it to school, and every kid in the class made a valentine for every member of the class and dropped them in the box ahead of time. On Valentine's Day we opened the box and handed out the valentines that we had made for each of our classmates to open. Everyone got the same number of valentines. Even though the valentines were homemade, it was a lot of fun.

We only had one Easter Egg Hunt at school and that was in the first grade with Mrs. Willie D. Parr as my teacher. We each had ten eggs that we dyed and decorated at home. I remember my mother boiling the eggs, and then she put vinegar in several cups. She had a package of different colored pills that she dropped in the cups. When they dissolved, they were ready to dye the egg red, green, blue, yellow, or purple. We went to Mrs. Parr's farmhouse in South Grapevine along Bear Creek, after school the last day of school before the Easter holiday. The eggs were all hidden by our parents in various places, some hard and some easy, and then we all went running with our Easter basket to find as many as we could. I ended up finding almost as many eggs as I had brought. We ate a few of the boiled eggs with a little salt and pepper, but most of them we just looked at until we had to throw them away. Obviously, Easter egg hunting is all about luck and not skill. I wished we had had an Easter egg hunt every year.

127. THE NIGHT FIRES

It seemed like all of the big fires that I witnessed growing up happened at night and usually in the winter. Most of them were probably started by stoves burning at night to keep the place warm. The first fire was the Moon Mullins house that was just two doors down from our house on Church Street. It burned to the ground one night, and of course, woke us all up with the sirens and commotion. I remember the flames went a hundred feet into the air, and I will never forget the roar that the fire made. A couple of years later in about 1950, one of the two mills just a block south of our house burned one night. Dad had to get the garden hose and water down the roof to our house because there were so many live embers landing on the roof and in the yard. We were scared to death that our house was going to burn. The firemen had laid fire hose from the fire plug across from our house. We could feel the heat from the fire. We could hear the pumper trucks pumping water as hard as they could, and the night air was full of loud voices giving commands. My dad's brother lived just across the street from the mill; my dad walked down to check on them to make sure they were alright, which they were. We had two other spectacular fires when I was growing up, but they were during the day. One was the Donnie Chair Factory on Hudgins Street that burned on a Saturday afternoon and engulfed Main Street with smoke. The other was the Grapevine Mattress Factory on Dove Road and Dove Loop that also burned to the ground on a Saturday morning. All of these major fires were accidents and total losses. The Mullins house was built back, but the businesses were gone forever.

128. DRIVE-IN'S & SUBMARINE RACES

The downtown area historically had been not only the mercantile district the entertainment district as well. This is where the carnival, circus and the skating rink came to town, where the political rally's where held, where Santa Claus came with his sleight and reindeer, where the FFA students held their show. It where live shows were held in the Woodman of the World Hall and the Orey House. It is were the pool hall and domino hall was located across from our stores. My granddad Tate liked to go shoot pool every day. It is where the Palace Theater was located. Mr. Bill Guest was the manager there when I was a kid and he walked around with a flashlight in his hand and he did not allow any rough housing, romance, or any conversation. Then in the early 1950's the drive in movie crazy spread across America. The Mustang Drive-In was built at the corner of Dallas Road and Highway 114. It was named after our high school mascot. It had a large silver screen, a concession stand, rest rooms, and a projector room. You could park your car where you wanted to and watch the movie from your car, so set on the hood or spread a blanket on the ground. There was a speaker on each poll next to each parking space. You took it inside and attached it to your car window and turned up the volume. This was an improvement in many ways from the Palace because you could interact and talk without disrupting anyone else.

    The boys like to play pranks on the girls. They would go to the rest room and come back and try and surprise or scare the girls in some way. I remember one time a couple of guys came back with Halloween mask on and fur gloves on their hands and they started jumping up and down on the back bumper to get their attention and then they said us get um, and open the doors and jump in on them the girls screaming at the top of their longs. It scared them nearly to death.

We also had Lake Grapevine to visit on quiet evenings and watch what was properly called the "Submarine Races". Of course there were no submarines on the lake. What couples did was sit in the car or on a pier and talk and watch the sailboats and waves pass by. There might have been a little romance involved but I don't know that for sure. Some were lucky enough to have access to a boat and could enjoy the lake with a different dimension.

129. FLASHBULBS AND FAMILY MOVIES

In those years we had a box shaped camera for rolls of red film to be threaded into the camera. It s cylinder rolled when you wound the camera after as each picture was taken. When the roll was fully exposed, you rewound the film into its metal container so it would not be exposed to the light. We would take it to the City Drugstore to send off to have developed.

All pictures had to be taken out of doors to get enough light to make them clear. Then came the flash bulb and flash attachment. Flash bulbs came a dozen to the box. Each bulb could only be used one time. When the camera was set off it simultaneously set off, the bulb which burned out in a bright flash offering enough light for the picture to produce a good imagine. This was a great invention in the fifties and allowed families to start taking pictures of Christmas celebrations, graduation, and birthday parties indoors. Flash bulbs improved picture taking by a long shot. Then a few years later came colored film which was another giant step in photography. The colored film was more expensive to buy and more expensive to develop so black and white film was still used for general occasions.

During the time the lake was being built, and when my father was mayor, he bought a Super 8 movie camera to record community events and family gatherings like reunions. Dad was always taking movies and enjoyed it very much. It was hard to learn how to set the light meter to get the color just right. You wound the camera and then you pressed a button and the film rolled as the movie was taken. We had a projector and showed these family movies at night to great appreciation. We also got a light attachment that had two bright light bulbs that plugged into the wall receptacle to take movies indoors. These movies are a part of the archives of the family now.

130. APPLE CRATES AND ORANGE BOXES

At the stores we got products that came in wooden boxes. I have always loved those wooden boxes and the things you could make from them. Fruits and vegetables came in wooden crates. Apple boxes were the best and the heaviest wood. The orange crates were longer and had a partition in the center. I collected everyone one of these I could get my hands on. I would take them apart and use the material. I made all kinds of boats, cars, knives, planes, and trains out of the wood. I made my own patterns and used a coping saw to cut them out. I also made sling shots and boards to mount scout projects on. It was soft wood and easy to cut and shape. The tomatoes and grapes came in smaller crates that could be used to cut out Christmas ornaments or to make pictures with my wood burning iron. I did not have a work bench so I used the back porch instead. It was a part of the "entertain yourself" lifestyle we lived as kids. I still have my Cub Scout wolf, bear and lion mounted on wood from these boxes as well as my collection of knots that I learned to tie.

131. MAGIC AND A BAG OF TRICKS

As a kid, I was attracted to magic just as many members of the Tate family were well known as tricksters. I had a nickel coin I could make disappear and some other tricks that came with a magic set I got for my birthday. I never was good enough to pull a rabbit out of a hat or cut a person into two parts like the real magicians could do. I had some string tricks that I learned from the old men setting in the hardware store. Mr. Charlie Berry taught me some knife tricks with my hands. I liked to pull some of these tricks on customers. I had some Mexican jumping beans. I would make it look like I took some bean seed out of a bin and then say "Hocus Pocus" and lay the jumping beans down and they would start to bounce around. It made people scratch their heads. We used to play the three walnut shells and pea trick and see who could guess which shell the pea was under after they were shuffled. It was the attention that I craved as well as the unknown. People pulled a lot of capers for entertainment. Sometimes kids would put a rooster in a mailbox to scare the postman when he brought the mail but not me. I had a rubber band trick that I wound a stick around a rubber band and put it in an envelope. When someone opened the envelope, it sounded like a rattlesnake rattling and scared them to death. My granddad liked to put a rubber snake or large spider on some one's shoulder who would think it was real.

132. SUMMER LUNCH

My mother cooked three meals a day. In the morning a big breakfast with biscuits, eggs, meat, and gravy. For supper she always cooked a big meal. In the summertime we had a lot of vegetables out of the garden to cook, but dad and I did not always have time to leave the store to go home for lunch, so Mother would bring it to us on a tray. There would be roast or steak or pork chops with black-eyed peas, corn on the cob, cantaloupe, and bread with iced tea. It was like a picnic on the ground except we ate it off of a counter for a table. Sometimes we would get busy during lunch because people would go shopping on their lunch hour. We would stop eating and wait on them. Sometimes our food would get cold, but in any event, I always enjoyed those summer lunches my mother was so good at fixing and serving to us at the store.

133. CEMETERIES AND HOLIDAY FLOWERS

My dad was born and raised in Denton County, and he had relatives buried in Old Hall Cemetery and Flower Mound Cemetery as well as in the Grapevine Cemetery.

He assumed responsibility for hoeing the cemetery lots in all three places which every spring was a big job. Back then it was the families that maintained the lots and not the Cemetery Associations. I followed my dad around every time he did this and was familiar with the families that were buried there, their names and relation. I also roamed around looking at other tombstones and the messages on the stones. One I remember at Old Hall was "A light in our house has burned out, a voice we all loved is still." My Great-grandfather Will Nowlin is buried at Old Hall by his first wife Missouri Ellen Nowlin. My Great-grandmother Martha Ellen Tate Nowlin is buried at the Flower Mound Cemetery beside her first husband, Robert Mitchell Tate. Also buried there were my dad's two baby sisters, Mary and Maria, who died at three months and six months from the milk fever. They now rest beside their parents in the Grapevine Cemetery. A cousin that was shot down and killed in the Second World War had a stone at Flower Mound, but his body wasn't there. My Grandfather and Grandmother Bennett and Grandfather and Grandmother Tate are all buried at Grapevine Cemetery. We would cut flowers in the yard and take them to the Grapevine Cemetery on holidays like Mother's or Father's Day, Christmas, July 4th, and Easter Sunday. I used to look at these graves and wonder what was below that I couldn't see and what accomplishments and sacrifices the people had experienced.

134. MINATURE GOLF AND AVOCADO SEED

We used to make a putt-putt golf course in the yard with two or three holes in the course. We would bury a can in the ground for the hole, build up dirt and put boards in various places for obstacles. We had a putter and some golf balls to practice our miniature golf. My neighbor had a son that was a couple of years older than me named Sam Davis. He was playing miniature golf with me one day and looked down on the ground and found a green colored pheasant egg that had been disposed of from my incubator. He picked it and said, "Oh, an avocado seed," and before I could say anything he put it in his blue jean pocket and said he was going to plant it. I saw him later that day and I asked him if he had planted the seed. He started jumping around and spit and said, "That wasn't an avocado seed; it had some kind of dead birth in it and it broke and got stinky stuff all in my pocket and maybe ruined my blue jeans." I just got down in the grass and rolled laughing because I knew what it was all along.

135. THE NIGHT WATCHMAN

In 1907 when Grapevine became incorporated, the charter provided for the position of Town Marshall. An election was had and my maternal Grandfather Will Bennett was elected the first town Marshall. The Marshall became more romantically known as the Night Watchman because that was his job - staying up all night watching the downtown area and firing his pistol in the event of a fire. My Grandfather Bennett also worked in the post office and ran a milk business as well as being a cotton farmer. In the beginning he also lit the kerosene lamps located along Main Street at dusk and turned them out at dawn.

In the next fifty years several people served as the night watchman. I did not know my grandfather because he died before I was born, but the Night Watchman I knew best was Mr. Marvin Langley. He sat on a bench at Willhoite's Garage except when he was making his rounds. He had a clock that had a punch key on it that he would enter during his rounds to prove that he had done so. He also had a Billy club and carried a gun on his hip and another one in his boot. In the summer he often just had a tee shirt on it was so hot. He dealt with troubled boys and walked them home instead of locking them up. He did arrest some drunks and locked them up for the night. Mr. Langley got into a fight with a drunk on Main Street, on a Saturday afternoon. The drunk was trying to take his gun, so Mr. Langley reached into his boot, took his second pistol out and shot and killed the drunk in view of the Saturday afternoon crowd that had gathered to shop and visit. Mr. Langley did not own a car or drive. This was the only time a Grapevine night watchman had to use his gun. He walked to work and to fulfill his responsibilities.

We had a jail that was made from concrete that looked like a hut with bars on a window and the door. It had a cot inside and a chamber pot and nothing else. Town people can remember when drunks or mental people were locked up over night and how they used to scream at night and beat on the door. The old jail has been moved around from its original place on Barton Street and is now located at Main and Franklin Street.

136. CIVIL DEFENSE AND SPACE

There was a period after WWII, after Stalin died in Russia, that we entered a period that was called the Cold War. Russia Premier Nikita Khrushchev got nuclear weapons and was always threatening to destroy the United States. In a speech at the United Nation's he took off his shoe and beat on the podium. The United States had dropped two nuclear bombs on Japan to end WWII and knew how destructive they had been, and it was a fearful time. We had to practice civil defense drills at school and some parent's even built bomb shelters. We already had a cellar that would serve the same purpose. At that time families were organized into what was called the Ground Observer Corps of the United States of America. I jointed with my dad. We went to meetings and learned how to assist others in the event of such an attack. We got a pin to wear and a membership card. We also had playing cards with different kinds of Russian airplanes pictured on them, so we would recognize them if we spotted such aircraft overhead.

The United States and Russia were in a space race to put a man in orbit. The United States put several unmanned spacecraft in orbit. You could see the spaceships at night as they passed over North Texas. Sometimes my Dad and I would get up in the middle of the night just to see one pass overhead. They appeared as a star that moved across the sky from horizon to horizon. It appeared that the Russians had gained the advantage and that anything could happen with such power and a reckless leader. We were vigilant and paid attention at what was going on around us. Thank God a Russian nuclear attack was an event that never happened.

137. STRAWBERRY SODAS AND COMIC BOOKS

Our stores were just four doors down from the City Drugstore and next door to the post office, which I visited several times a day. When I was already at the post office, I might as well visit the City Drugstore. With a nickel I could buy a strawberry ice cream soda with two dips of vanilla ice cream. It sure was good on a hot summer day. I would usually go by myself and order at the counter then take it over to one of the tables and sit down to eat it. After the soda was gone, I would usually go over and look at the comic books. There were a lot of different series like Bugs Bunny, Donald Duck, Mickey Mouse, Dick Tracy, an etc. I was a comic book nut. I bought a lot of comic books and looked at a lot more. I didn't read them; I just looked at the pictures that pretty well told the story. Oh, I guess I did read them as I got a little older. They also had hunting magazines like *Field and Stream* and *Outdoor Life* that I progressed to as I got a little older and began to follow my Dad around hunting and fishing in the woods and streams. On the same shelves were what they called adult books with beautiful women in thin cloths. It was just an accident that I noticed them and out of curiosity looked through a few. I knew I could never buy one, but I was too young to know their purpose or market. I had to be very secretive and not get caught. Luckily, Mr. Roy Chambers, the pharmacist, was in the back of the store filling drugs all the time, and no one seemed to notice or care if I was looking. After all you had to know what was in the magazines to know if you had an interest in spending the money to buy one.

138. RECORD PLAYERS AND BARN DANCES

My sister was older than I by three and half years, and she led my way into the future. She got into popular music, for example, long before I appreciated it and learned to dance. She had a radio and phonograph record player in the living room that had records that you played with popular songs like the "Tennessee Waltz."

Some of her girlfriends would come over and they would listen to those songs. After a lot of begging, I got her to teach me how to dance. She went to dances at school, that I did not get to attend, but there was a barn dance every Friday night at the Rod and Reel Club out near the lake that I got to tag along with her a few times. I was ready for the new world that was about to come and to leave my childhood behind. My sister Sandra was very kind and helped me a lot to make the transition. Big sisters are a good thing for a boy to have.

William D. Tate

139. HALLOWEEN AND OUTHOUSES.

Halloween was not as commercialized when I was a kid. My dad and I carved a jack o lantern only one time. We did have a few tricks-or-treaters come by the house and we did give them candy. However, my sister and I were never allowed to dress up in a mask or costumes and go out to tricks-or-treat because my dad thought we would get in trouble. There was more emphasis on the tricks than the treat back then. As a merchant on Main Street, my dad knew what was coming because the big trick was taking soap and soaping all of the store front windows downtown. It took hours to wash them off with warm water. My dad did not look forward to this holiday. It was no surprise to find someone's outhouse setting in the middle of Main Street the next morning either. The town had a group of high school boys to thank no doubt. It was easy to see why my parents did not look forward to Halloween and the mischief that went with it. Halloween was promoted as a time that goblins and witches dressed in tall, black pointed hats, riding broomsticks, came out of nowhere and did bad things to you. Who wanted to risk that? The kids also egged the cars that were parked on the streets in the neighborhoods. This mischief was a lot more fun for some than the candy that you could get for free at the door if you just asked.

140. CRICKETS AND GRASSHOPPERS

One thing about a farming town is it attracted insects to the plants that grow on the farm. The cotton attracted the boll weevils that nearly destroyed the industry until an insecticide was developed that would kill them before they damage the boll. The wheat attracted the green bugs and the corn the silkworm. But the fields attracted other insects after the crops matured that did less damage, ones that appeared after the spraying was complete.

Those insects included the cricket and the grasshopper. The grasshopper hatched out first after the crop was mature. They were hordes of them. They ate the leaves of the corn and multiplied by the millions. After the grasshopper came the black cricket that also did little to the crop itself but bred and fed off

My Barefoot Days

the stalks of the plants. When the crops were harvested, and the plants shredded and plowed under, the insects came to town looking for food. The grasshoppers usually arrived in August and lined the streets and alleyways. They got in the stores and show windows. Without adequate food, they died, in the summer heat that made an even bigger problem to be cleaned up by the merchants. I used to get a brown paper sack and catch as many grasshoppers as I could, hoping that my dad would take me fishing. They came in all sizes, big and small and in various colors and descriptions. In late September or early October, the crickets came to town by the millions. They too got into the stores and merchandise and were crawling everywhere. At night they swarmed around the streetlights in giant clouds that looked like locus. It was like a plague each fall.

141. THE ANVIL AND THE MOLASSES.

One of the things that identified Grapevine back when it was a farming community were the sounds and smells. Millican Blacksmith shop, located in a tin building was on the north end of town across the street from the water tower and water works. There they made hay hooks, and plows and put handles in hoes and shovels and sharpened them so they would be easier to use. They also welded and made horseshoes and all kinds of specialty products. Mr. Millican built a three-handled shovel that was used to break ground for the construction of Lake Grapevine. They had a furnace heated with coal that got very hot to heat the metal. Then they could hammer the metal into its desired shape with a hammer on an anvil. On fall mornings when the air was cool, we could hear the sound of the anvil all the way down Main Street. Bang, bang, bang, a sweet sound like the ringing of a bell.

    We had B & D Mills that at one time was our cities largest employer with over 300 employees. It was started by Buckner and Deacon but was owned and operated when I was young by W.D. Deacon and his two sons Floyd and Erl Deacon. They manufactured feed for dairies and poultry operations. Located just a block from where I grew up, they were the first vertical feed mill in American and the first to deliver feed to the farm in large bulk trucks. They bought the wheat, milo, and corn from the local farmers. Vitamins, minerals, molasses, and proteins were shipped in by rail car. The products were mixed and then pressed into pellets or cubes for feeding the livestock or poultry. On hot summer nights when the mill was going overtime, we could smell the sweet smell of the molasses as it was mixed into the feed. It was not an offensive smell at all. These smells and sounds were a part of the heritage of Grapevine, Texas, as a prairie farming town.

142. DRILLING THE WATER WELL.

The City's only source of community water was the well at Texas Street. It was old and wearing out. There would be some surface water from Lake Grapevine when it was completed but that was several years away. While my father was Mayor, Freese and Nichols Engineering firm recommended that the city drill another Paluxy well at the corner of Hudgins and Main Street. There, a big rig set up and drilled day and night. The rig made a lot of noise from drilling through the layers of sandstone to reach the Paluxy sands. It was hard for people near the site to sleep at night. There were a lot of lights on the rig which lit up the area. When they finally bottomed out and tested the water, they knew they had a well. Then they had to lay pipe and seal off the well and then penetrate the pipe to produce good, safe, clear water. I followed Dad to the site many times to check on the development of the well. Of course, there was no guarantee that useable water would be found.

During the drilling, a sack of cement broke and was lying on the ground wasting. Dad bagged up part of it for me to take home to mix with water and to play with. This was the best part of the new well for me. I never had had cement to work with before. It was a lot better and a lot more permanent that mud pies. I tried to lay some brick and make a ring around a small pecan tree in the back yard. When that didn't work out very well, I poured a rather attractive solid concrete ring around the tree.

Finally, a good well with tasty fresh water was made. A ground storage tank was built on site, and the well produced for many years. After Lake Grapevine was completed and the water treatment facility completed, it was cheaper to produce water out of the Lake than it was the deep, Paluxy wells.

143. LITTLE LEAGUE AND BALLFIELDS.

When I was twelve years old, Little League Baseball came to Grapevine. Mr. Bill Cherry, a Braniff Airline Pilot, was my coach. We practiced twice at week on a field at the high school on the black clay that cracked open in the summer with cracks so wide the baseball would fall into them and disappear. You had to get a stick and fork it out. We had wooden blocks for bases to practice, but regulation sandbags for games. We had real baseball uniforms and played five or seven inning games at the high school field. I played shortstop. One day, I got hit in the head with a baseball bat by a player on my team who was warming up and not watching what he was doing. The bat put a big lump on my head. I thought it had killed me. It made me a little gun shy.

We won most of our games that year. I got to play in the All-Star Game at Lewisville at the end of the season. The next year I moved up to the Pony League where the pitchers were much faster and threw curve balls. I was a good fielder, but I could not follow the ball at bat and was not a good hitter. I was afraid that the pitcher would hit me with the ball, and I knew it would hurt.

When I came home after ball practice, I would be so hot and dry that I would not take time to put sugar in my iced tea, but would drink it unsweetened. I would have to have a whole glass full before I started eating. As a result, I learned to like iced tea that way and never changed.

Playing baseball as a kid was a great opportunity in a small town. People played baseball at all ages. It was a good sport to know. My cousin Lanny Tate was playing on my team, and we practiced together on the east side of our yard. I would play like I was a play-by-play announcer to add a little spice to our workouts. We would dream big. The sky was the limit. We wanted the gold.

144. MODEL AIRPLANES AND BOOMERANGS

My dad bought me a silver model airplane that had a short fishing pole with a reel on it and a small nylon twin tied to the plane. We bought it at the Fort Worth Stock Show. The plane did not have a motor on it but wings that rotated in the wind to give it a lift. It operated like a guilder. We used to take it out to the fields and fly on windy days. It would rise and fall in the wind current, but once aloft it usually stayed in the air until you reeled it in. It was a lot of fun and easier to operate than a kite. Somehow, I never progressed to the motor operated model airplane that flew for real.

My dad also ordered me a boomerang that we saw advertised on television. The boomerang was an instrument used to hunt with in Australia instead of a bow and arrow or rifle. It seemed like it would be easy to operate, but it was not. It had two sides of the same length, like half of a square. It was made out of wood and when you threw it, it was expected to come back to you wherever you were standing. I never did figure out the technique, because the boomerang never seemed to want to return to me when I threw it. I was always having to retrieve it like any other object. My dad did not seem to know how to use it either. I thought I might be more effective in hunting birds than my BB gun. It turned out to be a great disappointment for both my dad and I.

145. THE PARAKEET.

My Granddad Tate never had a pet while I was around. You couldn't call the hog he fed out each fall as a pet because he was being raised for slaughter. Many of the early pioneers brought yellow canaries with them so they would have some color to look at during the dormant months, but my granddad never said whether his family had one or not.

Then one year there appeared on the market what they called a parakeet, which was like a very small parrot. They were inexpensive and became very popular very fast. We even sold parakeet cages in the stores. They came in several colors: green, blue, grey, and yellow. My granddad bought a blue parakeet for my grandmother to have some company during the day when she was alone. It was a reminder of the early pioneers and their canaries.

The plan was to teach the parakeet to talk like a parrot. His parakeet's name was Joe. They started with trying to get the bird to say "Joe," but he didn't seem to understand what was being asked of him. I had a friend that had a parrot that talked. It would say, Polly wants a cracker," and it would talk to the dogs and say, "Bad dog, bad dog!" Joe stayed in the cage for the first part of his life, and even though every effort was made to teach Joe to speak English, he refused to say a word. Then at night my granddad started to take him out of the cage and set him on his head and let him climb over his glasses and peck him on the nose. They developed a relationship with each other that became a substitute for conversation. It made me want a parakeet, but Mother said no because she knew that she would be the one that had to feed it and change the newspaper in its cage every few days. She was right. I was lucky, I guess, just to have a small round bowl with a couple of goldfish in it.

146. THE LAST DAYS OF GRANDDAD

My Granddad Tate was always a cutter. He liked to wrestle and pop knuckles with you. He was a jokester and horseplayer. On the other hand, he was down to earth. He wasn't a person that engaged in a lot of chit-chat or idle conversation. He was earthy, a man of the land. He hunted and fished a lot and worked in the garden and large flower beds in his yard at home. He was the butcher at the grocery store which was quite a physical job in itself. I always thought he was in good health. Then he started having pain in his left arm when he reached into the cold meat case to place a tray or to serve a customer. He also developed some shortness of breath and chest pains. This was not all explained to me at first and I didn't realize the seriousness of his condition. I begged my granddad to go deer hunting with my dad and me that fall on a day lease. He was reluctant, but he agreed to go just for me.

    We would come in from hunting and find him in bed. I realized then that he did not need to be there, that he was in fact sick. We decided to come home early. I always felt bad that I had talked granddad into going hunting, though he knew he was not in any condition to do so. His doctor was Dr. W.H. Wyss who lived in Keller but who had an office on Worth Street in Grapevine and also made house calls. My dad told me that Granddad had heart problems, that he had drank too much raw milk and eaten too much fatty pork and food cooked with lard, that his arteries were clogged with plaque that restricted the flow of blood. This worried me a lot. He would have bad moments when he had chest pain, and he would have to put a nitroglycerin table under his tongue and stay still for a few minutes. The pill would thin his blood and the pain would go away. This scared me and affected me a lot. I didn't know whether he was going to pass out or die before my very eyes. I felt helpless. Even more so, I was told that there was nothing that could be done to reverse his condition medically. It was my prayer, my hope that someday before I was old and in such a condition that there would be some new medicine developed or medical procedure to help give a person another chance at life. These episodes went on for over a year.

Then one Saturday morning, in November of 1955, the morning after the homecoming parade, my Granddad Tate had a heart attack in the middle of the night and passed away just a year after his mother, Great-grandma Nowlin. We remember him standing in front of the grocery store as we passed by in the parade. It was the last time my sister and I saw Granddad alive.

This was the first time that I experienced grief. He was the only grandfather that I had known, and now he was gone just after I became a teenager. In was the third experience of death in just a few short years. The funeral was at the Methodist Church in Grapevine. I remember there were a lot of flowers and his friend and hunting partner, Mr. Ira E. Coats from Coppell sang "In the Garden" and "Sunset." I remember crying my heart out. For several years after that I thought I was having chest pain and that I had a bad heart. My dad even took me to see Dr. Joe Allison who said I had pleurisy, an inflammation of the lining of the lungs. It took me a long time mentally to overcome and outgrow the experiences I had with Granddad Tate when he was having chest pains. I think my feelings were just anxiety attacks or sympathy pain from the experiences that I had witnessed with him. There was nothing physically wrong with me.

After Granddad Tate's death, some of the grandchildren stayed with my grandmother every night thereafter to help take care of her and so she would not be alone.

147. THE COMING OF AGE.

The years began to pass and I suddenly started to outgrow my shirts and blue jeans during every school year. Friends began to comment on how fast I was growing and how tall I was getting. It did seem to me that things were changing but I didn't know why. I was getting acne on my face, a nuisance that made one feel self- conscious. Acne certainly didn't make you look any better. I had often shaved my father on Sunday afternoons, and began to imagine shaving myself, but all I had was a little fuzz appearing here and there. When my hair turned from my blond baby hair to brown there was a small spot on my right front side that didn't change and stayed blond. It was kind of a birth mark, I think. I noticed that no one else had this mark and wished that I didn't either. I brought some hair coloring from the drug store, and when I was at my grandmothers, I tried to color the blond spot but the color didn't match. So I colored all of my hair but it was too dark. After having to give a little explanation to my parents, I discarded the coloring as a solution and accepted that I was different. My appetite had increased, and I was eating everything I could get my hands on. Although, I was growing taller, my face was still thin and looked immature. I became more aware of my appearance.

I still had not paid much attention to girls. That summer I had been behind the sofa looking at pictures stored in the bookshelves, when I was climbing out over the sofa and I brushed against it and I suddenly felt a good feeling that I had never felt before. I lay there on top of the sofa for a few minutes to enjoy the good feeling. My parents had not explained to me the changes that I might expect when I grew up or anything about "the birds and the bees". I began to research on my own and ask a few discreet questions to older friends. I soon realized that I was just "coming of age."

148. LEARNING TO DRIVE.

My sister, being older, gave her the privilege to do everything before me, which made me very jealous. I was always thinking that I should be able to do the same thing. When Bellaire Subdivision was being developed and the roads cut, my dad took my sister there to teach her how to drive the car on the streets before they were paved. Of course, I begged my dad to let me do the same. Before it was all over, he finally gave in one day and let me have a try at the wheel. Back then you could not get your licenses until you were sixteen years old and had taken drivers education. There were unofficial exceptions to that in a farming community like Grapevine, because every farm boy knew how to drive a tractor and pickup when they were still in elementary school. There really weren't any law officers in town back then to give you a ticket, and the boys help was needed on the farm. I could see over the wheel and reach the accelerator. That is why I couldn't understand why I was any different from a farm boy. I was certainly a small-town boy whose dad had a Chevrolet pickup. I basically learned to drive Dad's pickup from the house, the one block to the back of the stores where I could park it without incident. Those were my parameters. I could not drive anywhere else. This is how I learned to drive long before I would get my driver's license. It made a lot of sense to be able to drive to work even when I was twelve.

149. THUNDER & LIGHTNING.

Thunder is the sound created by lightning and can range from a sharp loud crack to a long rumble. The lightning strike causes an expansion of air and a resulting shock wave, which is referred to as a "peal of thunder." It is usually associated with a thunderstorm. The study of thunder is known as "brontology." I always wondered as a kid, thunder caused lightning or lightning created thunder. The fresh rain was a blessing to us who lived in a community where the principal occupation was farming. It was necessary for a good crop to get adequate rain at the right time. Getting adequate rainfall meant dealing with lightning and thunder. Acts 24:17, "He did not leave himself without witness, for he did good by giving you rain from Heaven and fruitful seasons, satisfying your hearts with food and gladness." Yet the thunder and lightning has been noted from Biblical times as a sign of Gods awesome power and presence. Luke 27:26, "For as the lightning flashes and lights up the sky from one side to the other, so will the Son of Man be in his day."

My great-grandpa Will Nowlin did not swear or cuss. When he got excited, he said instead, "Why thunder and lightning" It was also a reflection of his amazement or impression. When the electric refrigerator came out with the ice maker, my dad gave one to my great grandparents. When he delivered it and got it hooked up and showed Grandpa Nowlin how it would make ice in the trays and the ice man would no longer be necessary, his response was, "why thunder and lightning." I wish I had that discipline to express myself in such a way that would surely be pleasing to God.

150. THE WILEYS

My aunt Lela Mae Wiley was my mother's only sister. She had grown up in the house I grew up in in Grapevine. She married a Grapevine boy and they had four children: Donald, Eugene, Bettye, and Annette. She lived in Fort Worth on Honeysuckle Drive in the Oak Hurst Addition most of her married life. Behind the house was a garage with a washroom and overhead a garage apartment where my two cousins, Donald and Gene lived. My uncle Dick Wiley was the first manager of the Grapevine Chamber of Commerce or at least the forerunning of the Chamber. He grew up on a farm about twelve miles west of Grapevine. They lived in the old Bennett residence at 507 Church Street, where Donald and Gene were born. Uncle Dick sold used cars in a partnership called Sellers and Wiley located on North Main in Ft Worth. My Uncle Dick was a distinguished looking person and very smart. He was well respected and a good example to me. He was the kind of person who always was "thinking outside the box." He used to go to Chicago and Detroit with friends to buy cars and drive them back, each driver towing a second car behind him. One trip my Uncle Dick was driving cars back and he got stopped in a small town by a local cop. The cop said, "I stopped you for running the red light back there at the intersection." My uncle said, "No, I beg your pardon. The light was green when I entered the intersection." The cop said, "Yes, it wasn't you that ran the red light; it was the car that you were towing." My uncle said, "Well just give that driver a ticket or throw him in jail." Of course, there was no driver of the second car. In the end no ticket was given.

Uncle Dick was President of the Fort Worth Anglers club when the U. S. Corp of Engineers was building Lake Grapevine. He was responsible for getting the Texas Game and Fish Commission to stock game fish in Lake Grapevine.

We visited the Wiley family often. Either we went to Fort Worth or they came to Grapevine. We took flowers to the cemetery on holidays. We always had Christmas at their house. We would have a large turkey dinner with all the trimmings, including dressing and potato salad and corn. The four children each had a standard prayer that they said before every meal. It was the only family that I knew that practiced this ritual, which was very impressive and very nice. About three o'clock we would start opening presents. The Wileys were very generous and gave nice gifts. The men used a pocket knife to open the paper so it could be ironed and reused again. When we were through, I knew Christmas was over. We would return home to a cold house after dark.

I liked to explore through their garage. They had a lot of fishing equipment stored there and a lot of good stuff that was well organized. The washroom where the clothes were washed was very unique. It had a drain in the concrete floor where any water spilled could drain away. It also had a folding table for the dried clothes. It had a different smell to it than the rest of the building. My mother didn't have anything near this nice. There was an outside stairway that went to the upstairs apartment. I got to spend the night up there one time and enjoyed the view around the neighborhood. My cousins were into short wave radios and had a lot of interesting things up there for me to discover and explore. There was an intercom between the apartment and the main house for the family to communicate with each other. I liked to visit the Wileys and explore around the property.

When I was about four years old, the Wileys and my family rented cabins at Lake Possum Kingdom and had our first and only camping experience at the lake. The cabins were small but nice with a kitchen for preparing food. I wore a life preserver and swam in the lake on the beach area next to the cabins. We did not rent a boat or get out on the water or even fish. I can remember it was a lot of fun but, for some reason we never did it again. The Wiley children were older than my sister and I except for Annette who was the same age as my sister Sandra. I guess the older Wiley children had outgrown such campouts because there was less for them to do. The Wileys enjoyed going to Creed, Colorado each summer for their vacation.

The Wiley's live in a big city where life was much different than I experienced in the small town where I grew up. We had a post office box and had to go to the Post Office to pick up the mail, while they had a mail slot next to the front door and the postman delivered the mail to their house. The mail past through the slot and fell on the floor inside of the living room. We had a cow to milk to get our milk, while the Wiley's received their milk delivered at least twice a week to their front porch by the Borden Company. Another vendor often delivered fresh bread and sweet rolls to the house the same way. While we could get hand packed ice cream from the City Drug Store, they bought a different brand at their drug store with different flavors, including cherry vanilla which I loved because my mother often made that flavor when she made homemade ice cream in the refrigerator. The Wiley's went the Gulf Coast snapper fishing and brought back some fresh shrimp one year which I had never had. We got the fried scrimp in a shrimp basket at a local restaurant, but not the boiled variety. Mrs. Wiley would boil them and you had to shell them and pull the legs off and then dipped in a red cocktail sauce. They were delicious. It was a lot of fun to visit the Wiley's and they gave me a good education about city life.

151. THE PLANE CRASH

I remember it was in the month of September 1947. It was a Sunday afternoon, and I was in the living room with the family. The front door was open. My mother was trying to teach me some notes on the piano. We heard an airplane overhead that appeared to be in distress and was making an unusual sound. The engine was sputtering and cut in and out. Suddenly, we heard the impact and the ground and windows of the house shook. We knew it was close. Then the fire alarm went off and we heard the sirens responding down to the other end of our block on East College Street. I later went to the crash scene with my dad. The plane hit in the back yard of the Hart place next to the Allison Clinic at 212 E. Franklin Street. No structure was damaged. The Stearman plane was still there and was broken in pieces. Adin Monroe Hardin, who worked at Consolidated in Fort Worth and who had survived WWII, was learning to fly under the GI Bill. He and his instructor were both killed in the crash. His wife, Eva Dee, gave birth to the couple's son a week later. He was named Roger Dean Hardin, the name his father had helped choose. Roger would grow up to become a gifted artist and wood carver, and I would become one of his good friends.

152. THE FIRST KISS AND SPINNING THE BOTTLE

There was a girl in my sixth grade class that I thought was kind of pretty, with dark hair and dark eyes. She didn't have much to do with me. I think she matured early. Her name was Jane Doe. That summer she moved across the street from where I lived, and I began to notice her more. I would talk to her in the yard, and sometimes she would come over to the house and visit with me. I didn't drive a car, so I was too young to date. I think she had probably had some dates with older boys, but she was not going with anyone. My sister was dating a boy named Shep who was older than she and had already graduated from high school. He had a car and one night that summer he invited Jane and me to go out with them to Dudes Drive-In for a soft drink. After we had driven around town for a while and dragged Main Street we parked in front of our house. My sister was in the front seat and Jane and I in the back. We were having a good time in conversation and then the first thing I knew her lips and mine met. I had never tasted lipstick before, but knew instantly it was a tasty thing. It was sweeter than molasses and plum sugar. I never was so shocked in all of my life or had anything feel so good to me before. It took my breath. It blew my mind. It told me that there was something better than childhood after all. It did not take me long to learn to kiss. I probably did not sleep a wink that night and was suddenly in love with a girl far superior to me. We continued to see each other the rest of the summer and over the next year. Then her parents moved to Denton and she was gone just as fast as she had appeared. Jane was a member of the Church of Christ, and I was a Methodist, so neither of us had any help from our parents encouraging the relationship.

The next year in the seventh grade we had a class party at the home of Judy Stinson, the smartest girl in our class who would be our valedictorian when we graduated. I did not feel the same towards her as I had for Jane, but she was the girl that my mother had picked out at my tenth birthday party as my girlfriend and always pointed me in her direction. This turned into a real coming out party because we played a game the girls called "spin the bottle." When it became your turn, you spun the bottle. We were all sitting in a circle. When the bottle stopped spinning, whatever girl it was pointing to you got to kiss. I learned a lot about kissing that night including the fact some girls kiss better than other ones.

153. THE DUTCHMAN

I knew all my next-door neighbors, and we were all good friends. There was an area to the southwest, about a short block away that was in the edge of woods that led to the creek. There were a few scattered houses in this area but the people that lived there were not as accessible as our next- door neighbors. Some of them we didn't even know. A lady and her daughter lived together. The daughter must not have been right in her mind because we could hear her scream sometimes at night. Not that anyone was hurting her, she just screamed. We never were able to put a face on this woman or know for sure what she looked like, but I would not have wanted to be caught in her neighborhood after dark. She scared me. Just five houses to the west on College Street lived Mr. George M. Barrager, who was a widower. He used to work at the cotton gin on Scribner Street. He tied the bales, and after each he chucked his overalls and jumped into a barrel of water to cool off. He was born in Saginaw, Michigan in 1856 where he wore shoes. When he moved to Grapevine, Texas he just kind of gave them up. He acknowledged that a lot of people in Texas never wore shoes even in the winter.

    I would see him walk from his house to town down College Street to Church Street by our house. I knew who he was, but he seldom spoke or even waived. He was known as the "Barefooted Dutchman." His family had arrived in New York in 1662 among the original Dutch settlers in America. He had a mustache and smoked cigars. He was sort of a private person but could be very personable when he did get into a conversation. He had moved to Texas from South Dakota after his wife died. He said the last time he wore a pair of shoes was at his wife's funeral and he borrowed that pair. He had no grudge against shoes, nor did they hurt his feet. He said he didn't wear shoes simply because "he did not need 'um." The difference between me and him was that I only went barefoot in the warm summertime. Mr. Barrager went barefoot all year long and even when it snowed, we saw him walk to town without shoes. We didn't pity him or look down on him because it was a choice and a way of life. I wonder what he thought of me and the fact that he surely saw me going barefoot in the summertime and walking the hot streets when the tar got so hot during the day that it melted and stuck between your toes. He knew who I was and therefore knew that I could afford shoes. He must have thought that I just didn't wear shoes in the summertime because I "just didn't need 'um."

William D. Tate

154. THE FORT MASON HOTEL.

Most of our family vacations were spur-of-the-moment decisions, and most of the time it amounted to a quick trip to Mason, Texas and the surrounding area known as the Texas Hill County. We considered it the deer country because we did not have any deer or wild turkey in Grapevine or for hundreds of miles away. My first stay in a hotel was at the Fort Mason Hotel in Mason, Texas. It was four stories high and had a lobby and a restaurant inside. It was across from the courthouse that had a clock that chimed on the hour and half hour. The rooms in the hotel had high ceilings and large windows with a ceiling fan for extra ventilation. I don't think I ever went to sleep that first night because it was very hot in the middle of July and because of my excitement at looking for deer the next day. I heard the clock sound out every hour and half hour. There was a car on the street that had washed into the Llano River in a flood a few weeks before. It was piled up into many pieces that were hardly recognizable. People were gathered round the car talking about the accident and the person that lost his life. One of those gathered was named Tate Dodd, the football coach for the local high school. I was impressed by his name that required quite a bit of discuss with my father on family history looking into the possibility that we were kin folks.

The next morning, we had breakfast at the hotel and then headed to the country, driving around on gravel back roads. Whenever someone spotted deer, we would stop, back up, and see how many were there and if there were any bucks. It was a contest to see who could spot the most deer. We did see a lot of deer in the brush beside the roads but only a few bucks. We drove down to Kimbell County and visited the James River Ranch where my dad hunted in the fall. I saw one of the tree stands where my dad had killed deer and saw the headquarters of the ranch and met the ranch manager. I saw things that I had heard about before. My dad was a good-looking man, and I found out his hunting buddies nick named him "Gary" for Gary Cooper, a popular movie star at the time. I am sure they had a lot of fun kidding one another. Gary was not a name that caught on with me. It was always "Dad."

We passed through a little community called Harper during lunch time. We stopped at one of the few stores in town that was a family-owned restaurant. Dad wanted a steak. The waiter said that they only had one steak left, so my dad ordered it while the rest of the family ordered hamburgers. When the steak arrived, it was an entire cut of round steak that weighed at least a couple of pounds and would have been enough for the entire family. In the afternoon the deer started moving again and it was fun to see them run away. We ended back at the Mason Hotel to spend the night and then headed home the next day.

155. CHURCH CAMP AND GRAPEVINES

For a couple of summers the entire family went to Glen Rose to the Methodist Church camp. It had cabins for the kids and sponsors to stay in and then a large building where the meals were served. Then, there were separate girls' and boys' bathrooms, so the accommodations were nice but had some age to them. They were built primarily of native limestone. We had classes in the morning and then in the afternoon we went swimming in the pool and played games. At night we had what you might call church, with some heavy preaching about growing up to be responsible adults. I had never been in crowds like that for an overnight stay, and it was interesting to learn how churches promoted their faith.

We went exploring one night around the camp. There was a creek with trees growing along its banks and growing on the trees were grapevines. Even though I was from Grapevine, and we had a lot of grapevines growing at home but, I had not paid that much attention to them. Some of the older kids knew all about them. We cut a piece off one of the vines, about one-fourth of an inch in diameter and about three inches long. It had a hollow spot that ran down the middle of the stick. If you knew how to pick one that was dry, then you could light it and smoke it like a cigarette. My dad didn't seem to object so I joined some of my friends in smoking my first grapevine. It didn't make us sick or anything, and I brought a few pieces as a souvenir, a keepsake and token of remembrance of my first church camp.

156. DOVE HUNTS AND CHIGGERS

After I got my BB gun and shot at a few sparrows, I was ready for something bigger and more challenging-like a dove hunt. You could only hunt dove in season, which was September and October. You could only hunt in the afternoon. The birds fed in the grain fields in the afternoon and then went to water before dark. My first dove hunt was over in Denton County at Mr Wiley Small's farm. He had a small stock pond surrounded by trees that was located near FM 1171. We went one afternoon after school. You didn't have to worry about getting there too early because the birds didn't start to fly until about five o'clock or after. We set up in the trees. I was very excited. I didn't know a dove from a meadow lark, so my dad had to point them out. When they first started flying, I soon learned a hard lesson in life. Dove were hard to hit with a single shot BB. My dad didn't have any problem with his 20 ga shotgun. Even though I didn't kill anything on that first hunt, I learned a lot and I got to hold and look at it up close what a dead dove looked like and so could begin to dream about better days. I learned another lesson that night when I started scratching and itching and realized that the chiggers had just about eaten me alive. They don't have any reservations on where they attack you either, not even your private parts.

157. SNOW AND ICE STORMS.

It seemed that it snowed or came an ice storm two or three times every winter when I was growing up. We looked forward to the forecast and would get up the next morning to a blanket of snow. The first thing we did after getting on all the warm clothes we had was for Sandra and I to go out and play in the snow. We would try and make a snowman, but often the snow was too dry to stick together. The *Frosty the Snowman* book and song were out so we really wanted to make one of our own. We made one good one in the front yard one year. We did not have any coal for it's eyes, so we used corks for its eyes and a carrot for its nose. We wrapped a red scarf around its neck but when we put the old straw hat on his head he did not begin to dance around, much to our disappointment. We sang the song anyway and just pretended which is what childhood was all about.

We always wanted mother to make snow ice cream. I would be the one that would take a mixing bowl and a spatula and gather up the snow. Then mother would mix sugar and vanilla flavoring to it and mix it together. It was really good ice cream but some thought that it was not healthly because the snow caught all of the dust in the air when it fell.

Sometimes rather than snow we got ice storms. We had one really heavy ice storm in about 1949 when the temperature dropped to about zero. The trees were covered with over one- half inches of ice and broke the limbs off and dropped the power lines so we were without electricity for a few days. It took a lot of work for dad to cut up all of the limbs that broke off with a hand saw. It made the trees look ugly for a few years until they got their growth back.

I had to go out in the wet and cold to feed my rabbits and also my chickens and to take warm water out of the house to pour in their frozen water dishes so they could have water to drink. They seem to handle the cold better than I did.

158. PENCILS AND PAPER

Once upon a time there was a man who was handicapped and lived in Santo in Palo Pinto County with his family but worked in Ft Worth. He refused a wheelchair when his legs weakened from a spinal disease, and he crept along the sidewalk on all fours. He had leggings made from old tires and a leather vest that he wore. The leggings kept him from getting concrete burns on his body as he scooted along the sidewalk. There was a coin box and a pencil sack sewn into the back of his vest. He reminded me of an organ grinder with a monkey whom I had also seen in Ft. Worth on a street corner. Neither one was a beggar. They both were businessmen. The man with the monkey played and sang for you in consideration of a nickel or dime dropped in his tin cup. The pencil salesman I often saw outside Leonard Bros. store at Second and Houston Street, sold pencils and paper. At Christmas time he sold ribbons to wrap packages with. He also worked at the Ft. Worth Rodeo and at the Texas

State Fair in Dallas and on Main Street in Houston, Texas. His name was Frankie Brierton and he made enough to help support his wife and children. Sometimes when the sidewalks were crowded, people nearly stepped on him before they saw him. I saw him every time I went shopping downtown Ft. Worth, which would add up to many times. That is why I have never forgotten him. Years later, Willie Nelson wrote a Christmas song about him that became a classic. It is called "Pretty Paper."

159. HOMEMADE CLOTHES AND CHATTERING TEETH

My mother was a seamstress. She had a Singer sewing machine that stayed in her bedroom; I have fond memories of her sitting at the sewing machine making clothes for my sister and me. She also made all of her own clothes, including her evening dresses for Evening Star performances. She made cup towels, aprons, and other things from flour sacks. She bought most of the material for my shirts at E. J. Lipscomb and Son, a dry good store on Main Street. Lipscomb's sold a lot of material as well as blue jeans, work shirts and pants, shoes, and all kinds of dry goods. They sold ties but they did not sell men's suits. Sometimes my mother would take me into the store to look at the material and to give me a choice of what I would like. My mother made my shirts until I was in middle school. I really didn't notice until then that my shirts were a little different, the collars a little wider, the tails a little longer. I started noticing what other kids were wearing and one day said something to my mother like. "I would like to have a store bought shirt." That was the end of the shirt making. I am sorry if I broke my mother's heart.

I was born at the start of WWII and many things were rationed during the war like sugar and coffee, you had to have a ration book to be able to buy certain things. I didn't realize it until later in life that all of my clothes growing up were made from cotton. The war was fought in Europe. Much of the battlegrounds there were in a very cold climate. When the war moved to the Pacific Theater, the opposite was true and the problem was heat and malaria. All of the wool had gone to making clothing for the troops and that left the cotton

My Barefoot Days

for us kids. Our parents had some warmer cloths that they had left over before the war. I always wondered why I was always so cold. I was cold in the house, and I was cold when we went to things like a high school football game. I would be so cold my teeth would chatter. I thought there was something wrong with me because my parents did not get cold like that. Even when I started hunting, setting in a tree stand before day light with only a cotton unlined hunting coat on, I wondered why I got the shakes so bad. I shook so much I almost knocked the leaves off the trees. What I was missing was wool. I don't think our parents realized that us kids nearly froze to death in those days.

160. GANGSTERS AND GAMBLERS

The first thing that I knew about gangsters and gamblers was when it hit the newspaper that Herbert Noble's wife was killed when she put her foot on the ignition to the family car and a bomb when off and killed her. The bomb was meant for her husband, Herbert Noble. They lived across Denton Creek in Denton County, which was considered a part of Grapevine because it had a Grapevine Rural post office address. Mr. Noble also did most of his shopping in Grapevine. He had one child a daughter who went to school in Grapevine. This was the beginning of a long war between Benny Binion, who was an American gambling icon and convicted murderer who established illegal gambling operations in the Dallas-Fort Worth, area with a group of well-established local gamblers. I would see Mr. Noble when he came into the stores to shop. But after they started trying to kill him, he had to change his lifestyle. They tried many times, bringing down his airplane, and even trying to kill him in a hospital. They chased him from the circle in Northwest Dallas down State Highway 114 one night with both sides shooting at each other back and forth. He drove down Northwest Highway and turned north on North Main trying to get home. There was a sharp curve in North Main with a house located in the curve. He pulled in behind the house and got under the back porch and escaped. There were bullet holes for years in houses and barns located along the route through Grapevine.

My dad was mayor at the time, and while they were building the lake in 1950 we saw him one Sunday afternoon in August at the Denton Creek Bridge crossing. My dad stopped and talked with him. He was a heavyset man and was wearing shorts with a strapped under shirt. He was driving a 1948 dark blue Ford sedan. He opened the driver's door to talk with my dad, and I saw he had a machine gun strapped to the door and there was a pistol in his lap, several long guns beside him, and another long gun strapped to the opposite door. In the back seat there were two Great Dane dogs. None of that mattered the following Saturday, when he opened his mailbox. A person was watching from upon a hill and detonated the dynamite that had been buried under his mailbox a month before when he was out of town. We saw the Lucas ambulance come roaring down Main Street to the Allison Clinic with what was left of the man. The word soon spread through town that they had finally gotten Noble. The blast blew the Ford sedan into such small pieces that were just stacked up like junk when my dad and I arrived at the scene later that day. We saw the wire running up the hill into the trees and saw the detonator that was left behind. On the ninth try the gangsters finally killed Herbert Noble.

161. GROUNDBREAKING AND DEDICATION

The United States Congress passed the Rivers and Harbors Act of 1945 authorizing Lake Benbrook, Lake Lewisville, and Lake Grapevine. When it came time for the ground-breaking for Lake Grapevine, my dad was serving on the City Council with Mayor William Floyd Deacon. He built a speaker's stand that was twelve inches high and about four feet by five feet. He covered the top with black rubber flooring like we used in the isles in the grocery store. The stand was then painted black. After the dedication, Dad brought it home and the garbage cans set on it just behind the picket fence on Church Street.

I remember the groundbreaking on December 4, 1947. There was a barbeque lunch. There were a lot of people there including the Mayors of Dallas and Highland Park and representatives from the U. S. Corp of Engineers who would build the lake. The men all were dressed in suits with ties and felt hats. The site was near Old Grove Park where my Uncle Arthur Tate's house had sat. After lunch the contractor fired up a big, yellow machine called a caterpillar Open Bowl Scrapers. I had never seen such a thing before.

I remember how startled I was. There was a lot of smoke that came from a big pipe pointed upward. It was a powerful piece of equipment and a powerful moment for me.

The big piece of equipment came to life and scooped up into its belly a load of dirt and then dumped it. That is the kind of machines that they used to build the dam. I was very impressed with how it worked and how easily it could take the dirt from one place and move it to another. We went out to the dam almost every Sunday and watched these machines build the dam a scoop at a time.

When the lake was finished, the dedication was held July 3, 1952 at the turnaround on the south end of the dam overlooking the lake. My dad and I wore matching, Stetson style, straw hats. There was a big billboard there for many years with statistics about the lake. The General from the Corp gave a speech and I remember him saying that with normal rainfall the lake would fill up in five years. I remember that because I was thinking what a long time that would be. After the ceremony we all boarded three Grapevine school buses to take us to the tower where the gates were located that closed the dam and caused the impoundment of the water. I was only ten, but was the mayor's son, I got to push one of the eight red buttons that lowered a gate. When I pushed it, it started a motor that slowly started closing the gate. It only took thirteen minutes for all of the gates to close. After all of the gates were lowered, Denton Creek started to back up with the next rain. We had been in a five-year drought, but the following spring there was a flood. It rained 15 inches in one day and night. It broke the drought and filled the lake up in three days. Cotton Thompson was in a boat on the lake that night as it filled up and described all of the floating logs and debris that he had to deal with on that historic night.

162. SHAVING MY DAD

My dad worked hard six days a week. The Blue Sky Laws prevented the stores from opening on Sundays. It was a day of rest. After Sunday lunch my Dad lay in the big iron bed and listen to the radio and read the newspaper. He liked to get me to give him a shave while he was in bed. I don't remember how this got started or how I learned to give a shave since I was too young to shave myself. I did what I had to do. I think I was able to do it because I had watched the barber give customers shaves when I was waiting for a haircut. I would get a wet towel, Dad's razor with s fresh blade, and the shaving cup with soap in it. I put warm water in the cup to lather up the soap with the brush, and then I would move it all into the bedroom. I would put a warm towel on Dads face to get it warm and the hairs on his chin to soften them. Then I would give him a good lathering with the soap and start giving him a shave, beginning at the side -burns and working downward, then the other side., leaving the front to last. I must have done a good job, or he wouldn't have let me do it again. Only once did I ever give him a nick or cut. After I was through, I would take the towel and wipe all the remaining soap off and dry his face. It became something that I did for my dad on Sundays, something he seemed to appreciate. It was relaxing to him on a relaxing day, a day off from the chores of life. Something small I gave back for all he did for me.

163. COTTON AND THE GARBAGE TRUCK

After WWII and the soldiers came home, they were looking for work at that time. We did not have a garbage pickup in Grapevine. Rather, everyone burned their own trash. Cotton Thompson was hired by the city to pick up the trash in town and take it to some gravel pits south of town, where it could be burned and buried. He bought a bobtail truck with a steel bed. He would come around on the same day of each week for each customer. The city was broken up into different districts, and everyone knew their trash day. We would set the garbage cans out on the street for pick up on that given day. It was hard work. Mr. Thompson had to be strong enough to lift the garbage can over the side of the truck to dump it. He was a tall man but very thin. He did not look like he would be strong enough to do the job, but he was stronger than he looked.

He had been wounded in WWII in the battle for France. After the battle medics were putting the wounded into two piles. One was a pile that they thought the wounds were survivable and would be sent to a hospital for treatment, and the other was for those soldiers whose wounds were thought to be so severe that they would die. Cotton told the story that he realized that they had put him in the pile that they were not going to try to save so he crawled over and got in the other pile. He spent some time in a hospital in Pairs until after the war was over and then came home on a ship.

One day Cotton had a load of trash on his truck on a Saturday afternoon. He was parked in the middle of Barton Street behind the Jackson Barber Shop. He was tired and did not want to take the trash to the dump, so he just set the trash in his truck bed on fire. Skinny Lemons had a shoeshine stand in the barbershop. He was also the Justice of the Peace at one time and was a local volunteer fireman. Someone ran out the barbershop hollering that the garbage truck was on fire so Skinny when running out the back door, took a garden hose and put it out. It nearly scared Mr. Lemon to death. He thought he was a hero until he later found out later that Cotton had set the fire intentionally and that the truck had a steel bed and would not have been damaged. After all of that, Cotton had to go to the dump in spite of himself.

164. THE OLD MEN IN THE STORE

We had a large heater at the hardware store where men gathered around all day and talked. For the men it was a diversion, a delectation, and relaxation. For me it was an edification, swotting, and illumination. This is where I got my backbone. This is where I got my motivation. There was Tommy Martin whose wife worked next door at E. J. Lipscomb and Son and who lived in Colleyville. He was hunch backed and disabled and couldn't work. He also had a speech impediment. He came in everyday to pass the time. He was smart and gave a lot of good advice. There was Witt Stewart, a retired farmer who lived on E. College Street. He smoked and rolled his own cigarettes. I remember his fingers on his right hand were stained brown from the smoking. He had false teeth and often didn't wear them, so he gummed his lips a lot. He, too, had seen a lot of life and had a lot of good advice and opinions. He was a good man. Nabby Thompson was a handy man that did odd jobs and sometimes helped with customers in the store if we got busy. His brother Cotton Thompson, wounded in the Liberation of France, had a lot of advice to offer. There was Oscar Thomas, a retired schoolteacher that lived in a two-story house on

Main Street and like to play tennis. He was retired but would go to TCU or North Texas and play tennis with the girls on the college tennis team. He also liked to hunt and fish. He owned rental property and lived on the rent, so he had plenty of time to visit and give advice. He had a teacher's mentality. Bill Yancey, an insurance agent and former councilman, would come in during lunch or during coffee breaks to visit. A.J. Harper had one leg shorter than the other because of wounds received in an ambush along a hedgerow in Germany during the big war. He was a carpenter and a cabinet maker. There was Tommy Edison who was at Pearl Harbor and who worked for Whiteside Butane. There was Willis Pirkle who was a large dairy farmer. There was R.C. Patterson, a former schoolteacher and school superintendent who smoked a pipe and was free with advice. There was Tip Johnson, a contractor who helped build the Grapevine Dam. Corbett Emery, who built campers, had seen a lot of changes come to Grapevine. There was Lloyd Tillery who was the Constable of Pct 3 in Tarrant County for many years. These are only a few of the characters that I listened to on a regular basis. The names of some I have forgotten. Many more joined the debate every day. Many of them had been in the war and had war stories to tell. Some talked about their younger days and experiences with women. Some talked about their missed investments, land that they could have bought for a hundred dollars an acre that it was now worth five hundred dollars an acre. They talked about the city and city government, and what they would like to see Grapevine become. They inspired me in many ways to make good decisions in life and to make our community a better place.

165. INCUBATORS AND QUAIL

I learned to love quail from hunting the wild ones with my dad and skinning them into a big brown paper sack in the kitchen. My dad bought me a round metal incubator to hatch quail eggs. Dr. Bill Wilkerson across the lake and Bill Hogue raised quail and had a lot of eggs to give away. I bought four young blue quail and they came by freight train, and I went to the depot and picked them up. I remember I had to make each setting with numbers, or drawings or marks to identify when they should hatch and to identify those that didn't hatch and needed to be thrown away. Some would be marked with an X's, some

I would draw circles around the eggs, some I would just put dates on them. The temperature had to remain constant at 100 degrees. You had to keep a small bowl of water in the incubator for moisture so the chicks could hatch. It took from 16 to 20 days depending on the kind of quail. I started out with Bob Whites but expanded into Blues, Gamble, Red Quail and Blondes. I also had some Japanese Quail that hatched in 16 days and when they were six weeks old, they were mature and laying eggs. I ordered hatching eggs from different suppliers in different states, and they would come by U.S. mail.

I built small cages to put the young chicks in. You had to keep them warm but not too hot and you couldn't put too many together or they would bunch up and smother or start pecking each other. So you had to keep them separated. I made these out of tomato and apple crates that I got at the grocery store. I usually had about 15 to 20 chicks at a time. You had to keep the ages separated also. I put marbles or rocks in their water to keep them from drowning. I really enjoyed watching the quail grow up and gain their plumage that identified the males from the females.

I also raised Ringneck pheasants. We had our own hens so we could gather pheasant eggs and set them under setting hens. The pheasant hens would lay but wouldn't set on the eggs. The eggs were green or light grey in color. We gathered the eggs off the ground and put them in a wooden basket that strawberries had come in. We had to turn them every day to keep them from settling. Sometimes we set them under bantams, and some time I put them in my incubator. Mother boiled chicken eggs and we cut them up with a knife to get the pheasant chicks started eating. We had some pens without bottoms that we moved around on the grass for the young pheasants to eat grass as well as manufactured food. B & D Mills made a game bird feed that I used.

166. RAISING QUAIL

I was introduced to raising quail by Dr. William Wilkerson, a local dentist, and prankster, who lived across Denton Creek in Denton County. He invited me over one afternoon to see his operation. He had a large house and a pen full of Bob White quail. He showed me his incubator and told me how he raised quail. Then he gave me a pair to take home. My dad had his Uncle Arthur to make me a small pen to put them in. I made a small feeder out of a tomato crate and painted it red. This way I did not have to feed them every day. I loved to hear them whistle in the morning and afternoon. Dr. Joe Allison, a family doctor, also raised all kinds of quail and he gave me some baby quail to raise. Once again, I made a brooder out of a tomato crate that was about six inches high. It had to be designed such that the quail could not jump out when I was watering or feeding them. I covered the top with screen wire and made a door to put feed and water in the pen. I also enclosed the back area so they could have some shelter. I put a light bulb in the pen to keep them warm. A small mesh hardware cloth on the bottom let the droppings fall through and kept the pen clean. I set the brooder up on bricks. The first thing I knew I was hooked with several brooders, and I was raising all kinds of quail. In addition to the Bob White there were Red Quail, Japanese Quail, and Gamble Quail. I ordered a pair of Blue Scaled Quail from a catalogue and picked them up at the depot where they arrived by train. They didn't do well and died after a few short weeks. I later bought some Blue Quail eggs to get my start. I had a round incubator that held about 100 quail eggs that I used to hatch my chicks. This was the best of all my hobbies.

167. ALLISON'S CLINIC

My first experience with the doctor's office was when I had the croup. I remember Dr. J.M. Allison taking me into his dark library and pulling a medical book off the shelves and reading to my mother about my problem and how to treat it. The second experience I had with a doctor that I remember was when I got ring worms. A stray cat had come up to the house and of course I fed it and it stayed. From this cat I got some sores all over my body that were itching and multiplying, and I showed them to my teacher. She said I had ring worms, so she told my mother. This meant I had to go that very afternoon to see Dr. Joe Allison, who practiced with his father in a clinic on Franklin Street. He confirmed that I had a bad case of the ring worms, but assured me that they would not be fatal, just uncomfortable for a few weeks. He gave me some medicine that stained my skin reddish brown. I put on each sore until it healed. Part of my hair was shaved to treat the infections on my head. I didn't want another cat for a few years after that. I would see Dr. Joe Allison many times growing up. I remember going there onetime during flu season and the building and parking lot's being full. He had one bed for overnight patients and mothers delivering babies. He had a black and white chair in the back room that reminded me of a barber's chair. You would set in it and he would take your blood pressure and listen to your heart and kid you about it. He had part of two fingers missing on his right hand, and he was always poking on your stomach with those stubs. He had medicine scattered all over tables in his treatment room that made you wonder how he ever found anything. When he gave you a shot, he showed you the needle with a cover on it to make you think that was the needle. It was so big, it would make your eyes get big and your breath get short. He also liked to descent skunks and then give them away. He walked to the post office once a day to get the mail and to go to the drug store next door. He got where he blew a duck call all the way from his office down Main Street, living up to the reputation of being a "quack" doctor. Actually, he and his dad were both very good country doctors with renowned reputations.

168. JUNE BUGS AND FIREFLIES

In the month of June every year, never fails, the June bugs suddenly appeared crawling all over the screen windows and flying around lights everywhere. They were large brown bugs, actually beetles that seemed to serve no purpose in life except to be caught and put in a Mason jar to watch a day or two and then release. They came out at night attracted to light, in order to feed and breed and to become a pest to any outdoor activity. They burrowed into the ground two to five inches to lay their eggs. To see them flying was not a good sign because they represented the mature stage of a larvae or grub worm that eats the roots of grass and other plants and killed them. When you saw the June bugs it was already too late. However, for me they were a lot of fun to chase and catch.

The fireflies or lightning bugs also arrived in the summertime to light the night sky. They were actually nocturnal beetles like the June bug though they did not look like beetles. Their bodies flashed with beacons of light underneath their bellies to attract mates or prey. I never could figure out how they did that though we probed and scrutinized everyone. They were not an impressive looking bug but were agile fliers. They gave off a yellow, green, or light red cold light. We liked to chase them and try and catch them with our hands or in a net alive so they would still light up. We also put them in a jar just to watch and admire when they lit up the jar. I hope we didn't kill too many that way, because to my knowledge they are harmless to mankind. Just a lot of fun for a boy growing up in the country looking for something to do on a summer evening.

169. ENTERTAINED BY THE PRAIRIE

The Grapevine Prairie was scattered over about eighteen thousand acres, with occasional farmhouses along black dirt farm roads with grass growing in the middle. The farmer did not travel much, staying on the farm nearly every day except on Saturday when they came to town for supplies and Sunday when they came to worship. Of course, there were exceptions to that with other things to do during the week for any given farmer or his wife or children. For the most part the children went to public school in Grapevine, and there were always school activities to go to. During harvest time they made a lot of trips to town to bring the grains to the mill and the cotton to the gin. The roadway to the gin was lined in the fall with cotton that had fallen from the trailers.

The businessmen and women and towns people had a habit of driving out on the prairie on Sunday afternoons after church and dinner to look at the crops. This began even during planting time to see which farmer was getting his crop in early. That all of it depending on the philosophy of the farmer, the Farmer's Almanac, the weather, and the moisture in the soil. There was a race and a prize to get the first bale of cotton, but cotton was the last thing planted when the ground was warm. This was for some, including my family, a weekly pilgrimage during the season to be able to carry on a conversation with the farmer when he visited the store. It showed a personal interest in the farmer. The visit really got exciting as the crops matured. You could tell from the rain fall and by looking at the crops whether it was a good year or bad year. You can bet for sure the bankers made this trip on a routine basis. You could tell who maintained their farms the best and kept the Johnson Grass, sun flowers, and other invaders out of the field and those that kept the bar ditches mowed. By the time of harvest, the casual trips were usually over because the farmer was too busy harvesting the crop to stop and talk. It was more exciting to see the trucks and trailers bring the crops to town and learn to which farmer got the first bale.

170. BUTCHER BLOCK AND MEAT GRINDERS

My grandfather was the butcher in the Tate's Grocery Store and after he died then my father became the butcher. I watched him and learned the skills of a butcher. We had a large wooden butcher block that was so heavy you couldn't even move it. This is where we did the sawing and cutting of meat. There was a large array of knives, mallets, cleavers, and saws that hung on the wall. We had a large black sausage and hamburger meat grinder that had various plates that determined the size of the ground meat or chili meat. A wooden plunger pushed the meat into the grinder to prevent losing a hand or finger. Finally, we put the ground meat into enamel pans that had been sterilized. The grinder had to be carefully broken down and cleaned after every use. For hygiene purposes we wore white aprons and white hats. We had a very hot water system that sterilized the equipment and kept it safe. We sold homemade pork sausage and used the seasoning that came from Morton Company.

In the meat counter we also displayed steak, chicken, pork, eggs, cheese, lunch meat, and butter. We had a slicer for the lunch meat and cheese. It was the most dangerous piece of equipment in the market. I never got hurt, thank goodness.

171. ARROWHEADS AND INDIANS.

My dad liked to hunt arrowheads with Huley Higgins and John Hemley and maybe a few others. They would travel to known Indian camp sites and dig for treasures. There were known sites in Grapevine. There was a Caddo campground near Northwest Highway and Dove Road that extended to the west to the creek and water hole and spring where citizens used to go swim. There were also a lot of artifacts around what is now the Grapevine Water Treatment Plant that ran all the way to the Austin Patio Ranch to the east. There were other sites along the hills on each side of Denton Creek and along and near the creek itself. There were campgrounds along Grapevine Creek where Sam Houston met under the cottonwood trees and made peace with the Native America tribes. Other sites were along the hills in South Grapevine overlooking Bear Creek in the Parr Park vicinity and following the creek southward towards Minter's Chapel and the Hugh Simmons farm and dairy. Oscar Thomas hunted arrowheads around town for many years and found a lot of arrow points. At least ten native tribes traversed the Grapevine Prairie for centuries to hunt and fish, to trap, and to trade. The Caddo in the east wove wonderful baskets, and the Pueblos from the west made beautiful pottery. They also traded with the Anglo scouts for tobacco, beads, blankets, and whiskey and with French trappers who were interested in their furs. When the first Scot- Irish settlers arrived here, they saw the lodge poles of the Native Americans still standing on the Grapevine Prairie. Bleached skulls and bones of buffalo were scattered everywhere. Wild herds of horses could be seen for miles along the horizon. There were still large herds of deer and antelope roaming the prairie as well as wild turkey and prairie chicken. It was a rich hunting ground for the tribes. The Native Americans lived here for thousands of years taking only what they needed and leaving the rest for someone else. They lived in perfect harmony with nature. The buffalo dung and lightning fires kept the prairie fertile, so the grass continued to grow as tall as the back of a horse.

    The Native Americans could make an arrowhead or spear point in just a few minutes. That is why there are so many left. They re-sharpened them like a knife, taking a deer horn and breaking off each side of the point to make it sharp and to give it a perfect shape again. The Native Americans were a part of the land, and parts of their civilization and way of life are still hidden in the soil today waiting to be found. I have Indian blood in me from both sides of my family. I adopted at a very early age the love that my father had for Native Americans and the pleasure that can come from finding a perfect arrowhead.

172. PICTURE STUMP

On the East corner of our house was a stump that was about two foot in diameter and had cement poured over the top. I saw a picture once that had this tree in it before it died. It was some kind of cedar tree. There used to be a tree just like it in the front of the Joe Lipscomb house next door to the east and another one in front of the Fielder house around the corner on Main Street. They were all very big trees with dark green leaves. When you are looking for them you can find one here and there throughout the town. . At any rate this stump became a picture taking opportunity for the family. Sometimes we would be sitting on the stump and other times just standing nearby. It usually gave a good picture of the house in the background. I do not know why the stump was not dug up and was left with a cement top, because I have never seen this done before. It was a landmark for our property. We often just used it as a chair when we were out in the front yard.

173. EVADING POLIO

When I was a child growing up, the greatest fear around was for a child to get polio, short for poliomyelitis. Polio is an infectious disease of the nervous system that caused death or left the survivors crippled, usually in one or more legs or arms. This was especially a concern after I started to school because of the greater opportunity to be exposed to the disease. We had a girl in school that had had it and was left crippled in one leg. She wore a brace and limped when she walked. Her left leg did not continue to grow and was smaller than the other one. If you got the disease, you were put in what they called an "iron lung," a large round machine that looked like a giant capsule. Polio was a very frightening disease. In the early 1950s, Jonas Salk developed a vaccine to create an immunity to the disease. It was developed from dead virus that was injected into the body and developed an immunity to the recipient. The treatment was inexpensive. The shots were given in a series of three. After the first you waited one to two months and then received the second shot, and then the third came six to twelve months later. The shots were given to everyone in the community that wanted one. I can remember that the lines were long. They were given at the Grapevine Elementary School. The whole family went together to get these shots. We also took an oral dose that was given on a sugar cube. It was a miracle breakthrough in medical science and a great relief never to have to worry again about getting Polio.

174. ENCYCLOPEDIA AND REFERENCE BOOKS

Back in those days when we had a pain or felt bad, we didn't rush to the doctor but got out a large book about four inches thick that told you everything you ever wanted to know about medicine, diseases, and treatments. I watched my parents use this book often to treat Sandra and me when we were sick. You only went to the doctor when you were having a baby or needed a shot or had a broken bone. I learned to do the same as I learned to read. It actually helped to settle my nerves when I figured out that I weren't seriously ill and that I would soon recover.

We also had a 15 volume set of the Compton's Encyclopedia, a set of black books that were nicely displayed in the bookshelf in the living room. These were the most popular books we had. They had almost any information in books that we wanted to know and a lot of illustrations and pictures. It was first printed in 1922 by Frank E. Compton and was a perfect reference for home and school. I used it a lot just out of curiosity or for school lessons. I found it an amazing set of books that I learned to enjoy and to use as a kid, giving me encouragement to learn and to improve my knowledge.

Then, my dad bought a set of books about Abraham Lincoln by Robert Sandburg and also a set about Robert E. Lee. I followed my dad in reading the books on Lincoln that first summer that we had them but never got around to the volumes on Robert E. Lee.

This was the extent of our home library except for children's books and novels. If we needed anything else, it meant a trip to the Grapevine Public Library.

175. DON'T EVER FORGET HIM

B. R. Wall A.K.A Benjamin Richard Wall was born in Grapevine in its historic residential district and attended the Grapevine College, the forerunner of the public school system. He kept a daily diary of a boy growing up in small town America. He graduated from law school from Baylor University and received Texas State Bar Card No. 1. He never held a driver's license or owned a car. His clients drove him to the courthouse. He lived on Franklin Street in Grapevine and walked down Franklin Street to Main to work. There were very few trees along the route, so he bought some pecan trees and hired some boys to plant them to have some shade to walk to and from work. He always knew the Texas governor and could walk -in and visit at anytime without an appointment. Once he was riding a train to New York and met the founding father of the Boy Scouts of America. Thinking that would be a good program for the boys of Grapevine, he obtained the first Boy Scout Troup charter west of the Mississippi in 1913. Boy Scout Troup 7 has been in existence ever since. He always carried a few nickels in his pocket. When he would meet me on Main Street, he would stop and give me a nickel and say "go to the drug store and get you a strawberry soda, something I would gladly do. Mr. Wall was a leader in the community and very influential throughout the state. He founded the Grapevine Sun Newspaper when he was nineteen years old. He organized the Farmers & Merchants Milling Company in 1902. He formed a partnership with John Wood under the name of Wood-Wall Realty Company He was Mayor of Grapevine for over 25 years and was credited with many advancements in the community throughout the Great Depression, Dust Bowl, boll weevil plague and other challenging times. He bought an interest in a restaurant on Main Street and installed a jukebox. The Baptist Church asked him to remove the jukebox because of the dancing that it encouraged, and when he refused, the rumor was that the church disfellowshipped the mayor for a while.

He raised five daughters. When he got sick, Dad went to see him and, as usual, I tagged along. I remember the visit. Mr. Wall was in the bed, pale, weak, with a sallow voice effeminate, and facing his last days. When we left the house, my dad said to me. "That is a great man in there, and don't you ever forget him. We will never see his likes again."

William D. Tate

176 HOBOS AND DARK NIGHTS

We lived only a little over a block from the railroad tracks. A lot of freight traffic came through. There were homeless men, or hobos, that rode in empty box cars to have something to do and have a dry place to sleep. They travelled to many places and got to see a lot of the world free. Every once in awhile one of these hobos would come up in our yard begging for something to eat. They would be dirty looking with raggedy clothes and desperately hungry for something to eat. They maybe had not had anything to eat for a day or two. They had to pass by several houses before they arrived at our house, and either the homeowners were not at home or else they turned the hobos down. Some people were afraid of the hobos and were afraid they might steal, but my parents always tried to help anyone in need and would always give food to a hungry person.

Sometimes I went to a movie at the Palace Theater by myself on Friday night. Walking home after dark down Main Street, I looked in the store windows wondering if some hobo or other stranger was inside looking back at me. It made me uneasy because I had read the comic book *Casper the Ghost* and believed that ghost and monsters existed. I could see down the sidewalk and knew that the Night Watchman would be setting in front of Willhoite's Garage and that he could see me coming. That gave me some comfort. After I passed the Night Watchman, then I had to pass by a couple of two story frame houses with a lot of tall trees in front and then pass through the shadows of Statum's Gulf Station in the dark. I knew I was on my own, so from there I would run all the way home in the dark, past the houses and trees, and climb over the picket fence and slam the door behind me as I entered the house. Safe at last.

177. THE BARROW GANG

I was born in 1942 after my dad had laid down his gun. If he had done so, he might not have survived, and I would have never existed. On December 29, 1932 my dad was working for Buckner's Grocery Store when word came that the Home Bank in Grapevine had been robbed. Kirby Buckner opened the gun safe in his store and pulled out a brand new 35mm Remington rifle and a box of shells and tossed them to my dad and said, "Go get 'um." He and Ed Davis, who also worked at the store, and Justice of the Peace E. L. Jordan headed south. On a dirt side road about six miles south of town, they noticed a car that had slid into the ditch. Ed Davis stayed with the car to make sure that no one came back and stole it, and my dad followed the muddy footprints into the woods. He came upon a person who began to run and failed to heed demands to stop. My dad began chasing him through thick brush and briars and finally cornered the man in a creek. My dad lowered the gun on him and the man said, "Don't shoot, all I have done is rob a bank." His name was J. L. "Red" Stewart, a member of the Clyde Barrow gang. Dad marched the man back to the car and recovered one half of the money which the robbers had already divided up. All of the varnish had been scratched off the stock of the gun and my dad's shirt was torn to shreds by the briars.

The other bandit escaped by talking a farmer into driving him to Dallas. After the capture, my dad was appointed a Special Deputy by the Tarrant County Sheriff on January 24, 1933. A few nights after Red Stewart was captured, lawmen surrounded a house in Dallas looking for the other robber, Malcom Davis, a Tarrant County deputy sheriff from Grapevine, was shot and killed by Clyde Barrow. He is buried in the Grapevine Cemetery. During this time Bonnie and Clyde were active in Grapevine. Having several friends here, they spent a lot of time in town. One day a report came to town that Bonnie and Clyde were headed to Grapevine State Highway 121. My dad and Mr. Davis got their pistols and headed that way to intercept them. At about where the entrance now is to the Grapevine Dam, they intercepted the car. My dad said that a lump came in his throat, but it wasn't the couple. On the Easter morning that Bonnie and Clyde killed two Texas Highway patrolmen just west of Grapevine, my dad, who was dating Louise Bennett, pulled up in front of her house and ordered her to get out of the car. That was all he said, then he drove off. The bodies of the two highway patrolmen were brought to Lucas Funeral Home in Grapevine where they lay in State. The line of people to view their bodies extended all the way down Main Street. Louise later told my dad that he was going to get killed if he didn't throw that gun away, so he put his gun away. My dad later married Louise Bennett who became my mother.

William D. Tate

178 MY OWN GRANDPA

In about 1882 Robert Mitchel Tate and his young wife, Martha Ellen Tate walked to Texas with their small son Arthur, from the town of Ooltewah, in Hamilton County, Tennessee. After arriving in Denton County, they acquired land and started farming. They had three more children, Earl Otto Tate (my grandfather), Clarence Tate and Lula Tate Ratliff. Robert Mitchell died of a heart attack in 1905, and Martha Ellen married widower Will Nowlin. Mr. Nowlin had been married to Missouri Ellen Nowlin, who had a substantial amount of Native American blood. The Nowlin's had originated in Illinois. They had two daughters, Myrtle Ester Maud Nowlin (would became my grandmother) and Cora Nowlin. After Missouri Ellen died, Will Nowlin married the widow Martha Ellen Tate. The Tate children and the Nowlin girls grew up in the same household. Later my grandfather, Earl Otto Tate married his stepsister, Myrtle Ester Maud Nowlin. They had six children, Gordon Douglas Tate (my father), Erman Granville Tate, Clois Tate, Dorothy Tate Barnett, and two daughters, Mary and Marie who died in their first years from the milk sickness.

My dad was concerned whether his parents actually got married, because he could not find any record of a marriage license. He started to investigate but could not find a marriage license. He was asking questions to various family members. His uncle Arthur final said to him, "Gordon just let it go because it doesn't matter now," and so he did. It was confusing and my dad often liked to say because his father and mother were stepsister and brother that he thought that he was his own grandpa. I noticed that my dad resembled Grandpa Nowlin in the face, and I wondered what I would look like when I grew up, if I would resemble either one.

Martha Ellen worked on the farm in Tennessee and married when she was a teenager. She did not have the opportunity to get an education. She lived to be 92 years old. She lived through the Civil War, World War I, and World War II. She was a good cook and raised four children. She never read the Bible or a newspaper or a recipe. She never wrote a letter or signed her name. Like thirty percent to the people of her generation, Martha Ellen was illiterate. She never had a driver's license or owned a car. She lived to see the invention of the steel plow, the thrasher, the combine, the gasoline tractor, the telephone, the automobile, the airplane, the electric refrigerator, the gas cook stove, and the atomic bomb. Though there were dug water wells and outhouses in the backyards when she died, she had indoor plumbing. Her house was a wood frame house built around a log cabin with a dog run down the middle. Her offspring would become doctors, lawyers, teachers, and politicians, all of which marks how far we have come as a society.

179. JUNIOR HIGH

The junior high school building was a cut down version of the old abandoned high school. The second floor and the ground floor remodeled. It sat next to the elementary school building. It had four classrooms. There were two for the seventh grade and two for the eighth grade. We had several teachers now and they came to us to teach in what they called a home room. I liked the variety that the multi teacher system brought to education. Junior High was also the beginning of school sports. It was my introduction to the jockey strap. My dad explained it to me and sent me to E. J. Lipscomb & Sons dry good store to purchase one. I played football and basketball both years in junior high. I had grown tall but had not filled out and was somewhat clumsy and not very athletic. I didn't start in seventh grade but got to play off the bench. The workout uniforms and equipment had been handed down from several years and were in poor condition. The game uniforms were better, and I enjoyed being assigned a number. In football I called the plays and played in the backfield.

I was still reeling from the death of Granddad Tate and worried I was going to die of a heart attack. Though, I always was afraid I would fail my physical for playing sports. The girl next door had moved to Denton, and that made two voids in my life. I was in a recovery mode. In the 8th grade I began to get my confidence back and was a little more physical but still had some growing to do. I had a breakaway game in basketball at a tournament at Bedford Boys Ranch, and after that I began to score a lot. I had spent so many years preparing myself by practicing. I was amazed how much confidence added to my ability to perform.

William D. Tate

We had a junior high dance that I went to each year and tried my luck with the girls. My sister had taught me how to dance, but I was all over the girls' feet and shoes. It took me a while between dances to pick out another girl and get enough nerve to ask her if she would like to dance. Of course, the girls never turned anyone down. I was still a little clumsy and a little reserved. I still wanted to be a good athlete because I knew my father had been a good basketball and football player when he was in school at Old Donald and at Grapevine High School, and I recognized the stardom that high school athletes enjoyed in the community. The junior high years pasted quickly, and they were soon over. I remember graduating from junior high in the old gym, walking down the aisle and across the stage to get my diploma in the presence of my proud parents, realizing that some of the best years of my life were just ahead.

The seventh grade was the first time that a student could participate in the band program. My mother coming from a musical family wanted me to be able to play an instrument. I had already failed at the piano, so she thought maybe I would like to play another instrument. We went to the band hall before school started and talked with the band instructor and looked at the various instruments. I picked out the cornet, and my parents bought one for me so I could be in the band. I learned to play the instrument, but I had the same problem as with the piano. I did not like to practice, and practice makes perfect. I was in the band program throughout the seventh and eighth grades but never really liked it because I was never that good and was always forth or fifth chair because I did not apply myself properly. I never learned to play a musical instrument properly. I had been given a ukulele as a child which made me want to learn to play the guitar. I tried to teach myself, but was tone deaf and couldn't keep it tuned.

I had a spot on the right side of my head that my blonde hair did not turn brown and left what was described to me as a birth mark. No one else had this defect and it worried me as I grew older. I use to go to the drug store and get some hair coloring and eliminate this defect in my appearance, but the coloring didn't last and it was not a permanent solution. I also started growing a little fuss on my cheeks and chin and started using my father's razor to practice shaving. I also started wearing ties and sport jackets. Ties were very narrow back then. I noticed that my dad had been wearing much wider ties but that style was changing. He never did make the adjustment. Ties were a popular gift for Christmas and birthday presents and I started collecting a lot of them. None of them were very pretty colors but were dull and simple.

180. RAILROAD AND DEPOT

The St. Louis and Southwestern Railroad carefully planned out the Cotton Belt Line through the cotton country of Texas, from Texarkana through Tyler to Dallas to Ft. Worth to Waco. The route came through Grapevine, Texas. It was the dawn of a new era. Where the railroad passed communities by like Estelle, Mustang, Tarrant, Dido and Jellico, they withered and disappeared. Where the railroad came, it brought new jobs, better markets and a brighter future. The railroad is responsible for the commercial buildings built in that era along Main Street. The refrigerator cars allowed farmers to ship their produce to distant markets. The railroad brought in vitamins and minerals to B & D Mills to be manufactured into feed supplements. Farmers drove hogs down Main Street to the railhead for shipment to processing plants. Cotton bales filled the plant form outside the station in the fall for shipment to textile mills. The railroad brought lumber to Cameron Lumber Company and merchandise to retail stores. The railroad moved military equipment during times of war and men and women arrived home by rail after World Wars I and II. The trains carried the mail and slowed up as it passed the station to hang the mail bag on a hook. The railroad has been important to the development of our community and its economy.

The depot was where you shipped goods and purchased tickets to ride on the trains. It had a telegraph office for sending messages. It had a waiting room for passengers to get out of the cold or hot weather. It was a center of community life. It is where the station manager had their office. There is a bullet hole in the north wall of the depot from a gun fired by an exuberant citizen during a street dance, celebrating the end to World War I.

William D. Tate

181. BAREFOOT DAYS AND SANDBURRS.

In my growth years it seemed like by the summer recess from school that my shoes were getting a little tight and that I had outgrown them, not to mention that they were worn out. This was before thongs and sandals. It didn't make a lot of sense to buy a new pair of shoes for the summer because I would just wear them out and I would have to have another new pair when school started anyway. I enjoyed the freedom that came with being shoeless. The summers were hot, and we only had fans to cool the house. My feet sweated a lot. It was cooler barefoot. At the beginning of summer I would look at my feet and see how white and tender they were, but knew it wouldn't be too long until they were tough as steel with calluses behind every toe. It was not a new idea because I had often gone barefoot in the summertime before I started to school. The county patched the streets in the summertime putting hot tar in the cracks or overlaying the streets with a blanket of tar and topped off with pea gravel. In the middle of the day in a 100-degree heat the tar would melt and stick to your feet. Think about that because that was another reason to go barefoot. The tar would have absolutely ruined a pair of shoes. It didn't bother the adults who drove the cars, just the kids who had to walk the streets to get where they were going. The tar would burn a little but when mixed with sand it soon rubbed off.

We also had a lot of goat heads that grew in the yard and along the road right of ways. The horns would penetrate your feet and you would have to stop and pull them out. Otherwise you couldn't walk. This was the worst part of going barefoot. I only went barefoot for four or five summers. Then I was working more at the stores and had to wear shoes, so my summer shoes became black tennis shoes. I am sure that my dad's generation didn't wear shoes a lot of the time and went barefoot, primarily because of the frugal lifestyle and the "make do" attitude of the prairie farmer. My mother did not want any pictures taken with me barefoot, because she was afraid that those that saw them would think that we were poor, which was not the case.

My childhood days were simple and gentle, full of life and imagination, a time when I found my wings, and spent my days as free as a sparrow. It was a time when I would begin to forsake the husbandry and agronomy roots of my family for something more substantial and to prepare myself for a boisterous and "rough and tumble" way of life that the future would surely bring. I was committed to learning the nitty-gritty and all the essential elements of leadership and governance not only to improve myself, but to influence the success of others, and to better our community. I accepted the unsolicited challenge of fulfilling the unfinished dreams of the old men who spent their time in my father's store, energized by the motivation and encouragement that they gave me in my barefoot days.

Will and Etta Bennett, Lela Mae

Grandfather Bennett

"My sister Sandra and I and our outdoor bedroom

Sister Sandra showing our backyard and the big tree

My Barefoot Days

Bill in Scout uniform

2016

Lela Mae Wiley

Dick Wiley

Betty and William and all of their grandchildren

My family on our 50th wedding anniversary cruise

Tate Grocery

Back: Aunt Dollie, Uncle Arthur, Grandad and Grandma Tate
Front: Grandma Nowlin and Grandpa Nowlin

Groundbreaking for Lake Grapevine

Cousin Lanny Tate and me

Gordon Tate as Special Deputy

William D. Tate

Me and Cousin Gene Wiley

William D. Tate

My Barefoot Days

William D. Tate

My Barefoot Days

Cowboy Clothes bought from Ceral boxes

My Barefoot Days

Dad with basketball goal

Back: Uncle Erman and Uncle Clois Tate
Front: Grandad Tate, Aunt Dorothy, Mur and Dad

THIS IS TO CERTIFY THAT

_____

HAS SUCCESSFULLY COMPLETED THE ___GOC OBSERVATION POST___ TRAINING COURSE ADMINISTERED BY THE UNITED STATES AIR FORCE, AND IS FULLY QUALIFIED TO PERFORM THOSE DUTIES AS A VOLUNTEER MEMBER OF THE GROUND OBSERVER CORPS OF THE UNITED STATES OF AMERICA.

Dated this __25th__ day of __April__, 19__56__.

ROBERT J. ARMSTRONG, Capt., USAF
Detachment Commander

E. E. Partridge
General, USAF
Commander
Air Defense Command

FORT WORTH, TEXAS, __Jan 24, 1933__

MR. __GORDON TATE__

HAS BEEN COMMISSIONED AS

Special Deputy Sheriff

SHERIFF TARRANT COUNTY

THIS COMMISSION EXPIRES __Dec. 31, 1934__

Mother and back porch

Front row: Dollie and Charlie Berry back their 4 children

My Barefoot Days

William D. Tate

Me and my dog Jerry

William D. Tate

My Barefoot Days

William D. Tate

My Barefoot Days

William D. Tate

My Barefoot Days

Birthday Cake

William D. Tate

Dressing Up

My Barefoot Days

William D. Tate

My Barefoot Days

Dad, Sandra and I at Methodist camp

William D. Tate

Printed in the USA
CPSIA information can be obtained
at www.ICGtesting.com
LVHW010217310724
786664LV00011B/405